DORLING KINDERSLEY DK EYEWITNESS GUIDES

FOOD

Stir-frying – a healthy
cooking method

Chocolate – a source of iron

Apples and cranberries –
rich in soluble fibre

Lobster – from the
crustacean family

Olive oil – a type of
monounsaturated fat

Fresh fruit –
full of antioxidants

EYEWITNESS GUIDES

FOOD

Written by
LAURA BULLER

Buddhist monks eating vegetarian food

Potato plant

LONDON, NEW YORK, MELBOURNE,
MUNICH, AND DELHI

For Cooling Brown Ltd:
Creative director Arthur Brown
Project editor Kesta Desmond
Senior designer Tish Jones
Designers Elaine Hewson, Elly King

For Dorling Kindersley Ltd:
Senior editor David John
Project art editor Philip Letsu
Managing editor Linda Esposito
Managing art editor Jane Thomas
Publishing manager Andrew Macintyre
Publishing director Jonathan Metcalf
Picture researcher Marie Ortu
Picture librarians Sarah Mills, Kate Ledwith
Production controller Luca Bazzoli
DTP designer Natasha Lu
Jacket designer Karen Shooter
Consultant Fiona Hunter

This Eyewitness ® Guide has been conceived by
Dorling Kindersley Limited and Editions Gallimard

First published in Great Britain in 2005 by
Dorling Kindersley Limited,
80 Strand, London WC2R 0RL

2 4 6 8 10 9 7 5 3 1

Copyright © 2005 Dorling Kindersley Limited, London
Penguin Group

A CIP catalogue record for this book is available from the British Library.

ISBN 1 4053 0833 8

Colour reproduction by Colourscan, Singapore
Printed in China by Toppan Printing Co.,
(Shenzhen) Ltd

Peppers – rich in
phytochemicals

Old-
fashioned
calorimeter

Sweets with artificial
colouring

Pickled
foods

Oily fish – rich in
essential fatty acids

Discover more at
www.dk.com

Contents

Vegetarian food

The web of life

THE FLOW OF ENERGY FROM THE SUN to plants to plant eaters to meat eaters is described as the food chain. At the base of the food chain are the primary producers – green plants and certain types of bacteria and algae. They use the sun's energy to make food, which they store in their cells. Plant-eating animals (herbivores) are the primary consumers in the food chain. They eat plants to get the energy that they need to live. Herbivores in turn are eaten by meat-eaters (carnivores), the secondary consumers in the food chain. Most animals are part of more than one food chain, and eat more than one kind of food – the term "food web" is often used to describe the complex way in which animals depend upon plants and each other for food.

HERE COMES THE SUN
With a few exceptions, all the energy for life comes from the sun. The sun floods the Earth with radiant energy in the form of sunlight. Green plants and certain types of bacteria can make food with sunlight, carbon dioxide, and water by a process known as photosynthesis.

A PYRAMID OF ENERGY
Food chains work in a pyramid shape with many plants at the bottom and just a few carnivores at the top. This is because the further up the food chain you go, the less food (and hence energy) remains available. A food chain cannot have more than four or five links, because there would not be enough food for animals at the top of the chain to stay alive.

Fox eats rabbits to get energy stored in their body cells

Rabbits eat grass for its stores of glucose

HUMANS
Like other animals, we are consumers in a food web. We belong to a group called omnivores, who get energy from both plants and animals.

Green plants make and store glucose (sugar)

THE FOOD WEB

Most animals belong to more than one food chain, interconnected with others. Interconnected food chains form a food web. This illustration shows how plants and animals feed off one another in a typical food web of a woodland lake. The arrows are drawn from the food consumer to the food source. The balance of plant and animal life within a food web is crucial. A change in the size of one population in the web will affect the other populations.

SNAKE

The snake opens its hinged jaw wide enough to swallow the frog whole. It is a secondary consumer in this particular food web.

EAGLE

This bird means business when it swoops down to catch its prey – salamanders, trout, and snakes are all on the menu. The eagle is a secondary consumer in the food web.

SALAMANDER

A salamander gobbles up a dragonfly. It is a secondary consumer.

TROUT

This fish eats phytoplankton and dragonflies. It is a primary consumer in the food web.

DRAGONFLY

This insect eats phytoplankton. Dragonflies are primary consumers in the food web.

FROG

The frog eats the dragonfly, which makes it another secondary consumer in the food web.

PHYTOPLANKTON

Small green organisms called phytoplankton (left) use sunlight, carbon dioxide, and water to make glucose and other molecules that animals can eat. Phytoplankton are primary producers.

THE DECOMPOSERS

The outsiders in a food web are the decomposers. They are mostly bacteria and fungi, as well as maggots, worms, and dung beetles. They eat dead plants and animals to get every last bit of energy. Without them, the Earth would be littered with dead things.

What is food?

FOOD IS ENERGY for life. We need food to provide the fuel that enables us to move and keep warm. Food also provides the essential materials that we need to build, repair, and maintain our body tissues and organs, and keep us healthy. The substances in food that accomplish these functions are called nutrients. There are two main categories of nutrient: macronutrients (including carbohydrates, protein, and fats), which are the basic building blocks of nutrition, and micronutrients (vitamins and minerals). We need to eat plenty of macronutrients in our daily diet, whereas micronutrients, although essential, are needed in much smaller amounts. Water is not normally considered a nutrient, but it is a basic component of all foods, and is essential to life.

Bread provides carbohydrates

Meat is an excellent source of protein

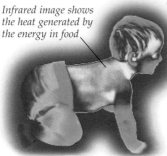

Infrared image shows the heat generated by the energy in food

THE HUMAN BODY
The matter that makes up each cell of the human body (apart from the cells produced before birth) is obtained from food. Children need relatively large amounts of nutrients because they grow so rapidly – a baby may triple in weight in its first year.

A SOURCE OF ENERGY
Food gives us the power we need to get up and go. Our bodies are constantly burning a mixture of macronutrients for energy that enables us to be active. Even when we are resting, we need energy to keep our lungs working, our hearts beating, and other essential body processes ticking over.

Eggs are a vegetarian source of protein

Bananas are a good source of the mineral potassium

OUR DAILY DIET
To maintain good health, we need to eat a well-balanced diet that contains an adequate but not excessive amount of carbohydrates, proteins, and fat. They are the chief source of energy for body functioning and muscle activity. Eating a wide variety of fresh foods, particularly fruit and vegetables, helps to ensure we get the vitamins and minerals that scientists know we need for good health – as well as those that have not yet been identified.

Dried fruit is a good vitamin- and mineral-rich snack

Nuts supply vitamin E

WATER WORKS
We can survive for weeks without food but only a few days without water. It is the main ingredient of blood and it carries waste products out of the body. Because we lose water all the time (when we urinate, perspire, or exhale, for example) we need to drink frequently. The average adult needs about 1–1.5 litre (2–2.5 pints) of fluid a day.

BRAN FIBRE
Foods such as bran are rich in fibre. This is the part of plant foods that we cannot digest. Strictly speaking, fibre is not a nutrient but it still plays a role in keeping us healthy.

Dried peas and beans are a good vegetarian source of the mineral iron

Micrograph of vitamin C crystal

VITAMINS AND MINERALS
Our bodies cannot make all of the vitamins we need, so we must obtain them from the foods we eat. Vitamins are important to human metabolism. Minerals are found in the environment but we cannot make them. We need to eat plants and meat that have absorbed minerals.

Green, leafy vegetables are full of vitamins and minerals

THE RIGHT NUTRITION
In areas affected by natural disaster, poverty, or war, it may be difficult to get enough food to eat, or enough of the right types of foods. This has a negative effect on health. Food aid programmes exist to help people, like these Angolan children, meet basic nutritional needs.

Fish provide healthy fats

Calories

Crave them, count them, or cut them, we all need a certain number of calories to provide us with energy through the day. The amount of calories in food is the measure of how much potential energy a food contains. This varies depending on the type of food. For example, a gram (0.03oz) of carbohydrate or protein contains 4 calories, and a gram of fat contains 9. Exactly how many calories we need every day depends on our height, weight, age, gender, and activity levels. In general, adult men need about 2,500 calories a day and adult women need about 2,000 (children need fewer).

ANTOINE LAVOISIER (1743–94)
French scientist Lavoisier, known as the father of modern chemistry, studied the role of oxygen in animal respiration. Lavoisier established a theory that heat consists of a substance he called "caloric", which could be transferred from one thing to another, but not created or destroyed.

Thermometers

Late 19th-century gas calorimeter

Food is burned in an inner chamber

Gas goes in here

Skin fold calipers measure body fat

TOO MANY CALORIES
We burn calories by breaking them down through metabolism (chemical processes in the body). If we consume more calories than we can burn, the excess is stored as fat. For example, if we consume 3,500 calories in excess of our needs, this is stored on the body as 0.5kg (1lb) of fat. Being overweight is associated with serious health risks.

MEASURING THE ENERGY VALUE OF FOOD
A calorimeter is a device used to measure calorie contents of individual foods. It consists of a sealed metal container, set in another container filled with water at a known temperature. Food is burned in the metal container and the heat transfers to the water. The resulting temperature change in the water is measured and used to find a calorie value.

GOING FOR THE BURN
Physical activity burns calories, which is why it is important to balance diet with exercise. Light activity burns fewer calories than strenuous activity. An activity such as running burns more than 300 calories in 30 minutes.

50 cherry tomatoes

1 chocolate shortbread biscuit

1 large glass of orange juice

About 4 squares of chocolate

1 cube of cheese the size of a single dice

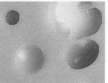

1 large chicken's egg

COMPARING CALORIFIC VALUES

Different foods contain different amounts of calories. Each food item on the left contains about 100 calories. A small piece of fatty food such as cheese shares the same calorie count as a whole bowlful of a non-fatty food such as cherry tomatoes. Whether fat, protein, or carbohydrate, a calorie is a calorie. This means that any type of food can be fattening if we eat it in sufficient amounts.

Pepsin enzyme

PEPSIN ENZYME

Calories are burned in complex metabolic processes in which enzymes (protein substances) play a critical role. Enzymes break down carbohydrates into sugars, fats into fatty acids and glycerol, and proteins into amino acids. Pepsin, an enzyme secreted by the stomach, breaks down protein into peptides (chains of amino acids).

Beer contains B vitamins

TO YOUR HEALTH?

Although alcoholic drinks do provide some vitamins and minerals, calories from wine, beer, and spirits do not offer the best nutritional value. In addition, excess alcohol consumption can cause weight gain over time – there are 7 calories in 1g (0.03oz) of alcohol.

Ice-cream contains about 195 calories per 100g (3.5oz) serving

Spirits contain 222 calories per 100ml (3.4fl oz)

Red wine contains healthy phytochemicals

Peak marks a heartbeat

THE BEATING HEART

Even when we are at rest, the heart is busy pumping blood, the lungs are inflating and deflating, and our other organs are working. The amount of energy needed just to keep us ticking over is called the basal metabolic rate. About 60–70 per cent of the calories burned in a day are used up on basic bodily processes.

COLD COMFORT

It takes energy to digest food, but some people mistakenly believe that the process of warming up cold foods, such as ice-cream, inside your body requires more energy than is present in the food itself. Sadly, ice-cream is far from being a calorie-free treat.

The food guide pyramid

THE FOOD GUIDE PYRAMID provides dietary guidelines that help people to make the best food choices for health. The one shown here was introduced in the United States in 1992 to help reduce the rising incidence of heart disease and strokes. The pyramid provides an easy-to-understand representation of what and how much to eat from each food group to get the nutrients you need, without too many calories, or too much fat, sugar, cholesterol, sodium, or alcohol. Following the guidelines will help to reduce the risk of certain diseases and make you healthier in the long term. Other countries use similar dietary guidelines, with similar proportions.

GUIDE TO FOOD CHOICES
The pyramid is not designed to be a rigid list of what you must eat each day. Instead, it is a general guide that lets you choose a healthy diet that is right for you. If you look at the levels of the pyramid, you will see that most of your daily diet should be based upon foods in the three lower sections. Foods in the uppermost section should be eaten in moderation. As you can see, you need to eat more plant than animal foods every day.

BASIC FOOD GROUPS
Before the food guide pyramid was introduced, nutritionists advised eating certain proportions of food from the basic food groups shown above, but advice was not presented in such a visual and easy-to-understand way. In addition, the guidelines did not address the need to keep total fat and saturated fat intake low.

Potatoes are a valuable source of complex carbohydrates

FATS, OILS, AND SUGAR
The foods at the small tip of the pyramid – fats, oils, and sweets – provide plenty of calories but very little in the way of nutrition. These foods should be used sparingly in the diet.

Olive oil

Vegetable-rich salad

Ripe tomatoes

THE MEDITERRANEAN DIET
Scientific studies have found that people in Mediterranean regions have long, healthy lives and relatively low rates of chronic disease. Their diet may be the reason. It is based upon an abundance of plant foods, from fruit and vegetables to pasta and beans. Fish and poultry are chosen in preference to red meats, and most foods are minimally processed.

MEAT, FISH, EGGS, DRIED BEANS, AND NUTS
The pyramid recommends eating 2–3 servings from this group daily. These foods provide protein, calcium, iron, and zinc. The healthiest types of meats are those that are low in saturated fat.

Steamed rice is a staple

DAIRY PRODUCTS
This group includes milk, yoghurt, and cheese. You should eat 2–3 servings daily. Choosing skimmed or semi-skimmed milk and reduced-fat cheese and yoghurt is best for good health.

Fresh vegetables

THE ASIAN DIET
Several studies indicate that people who eat a traditional Asian diet are at a lower risk of chronic disease than Westerners. The bulk of calories in this diet also comes from plant-based foods, especially rice, the staple food of Asia. Meats are eaten sparingly.

VEGETABLES
Eat up your greens – and reds, yellows, oranges, and browns, too. The pyramid advises eating 3–5 servings a day. Vegetables provide vitamins, minerals, and fibre, and are also low in fat. Dark-green leafy vegetables are a particularly good source of nutrients.

FRUIT
Fruit and fruit juices are low in fats and sodium and provide important amounts of vitamins. You should eat/drink 2–4 servings daily.

BREAD, CEREAL, RICE, PASTA
These foods are important because they provide complex carbohydrates, an important source of energy. The pyramid recommends eating 6–11 servings a day. Choosing whole-grain products gives you the fibre you need.

Choosing healthy food

WE ARE WHAT WE EAT, so why not eat the best? Experts agree that we need an adequate but not excessive number of calories per day, and that the bulk of these should come from complex carbohydrates, such as bread, rice, or potatoes. These foods are low in fat and provide vitamins and minerals. We should also be selective in the type of protein we eat, focusing on low-fat sources, such as lean meat, fish, and poultry, rather than fatty cuts of meat and full-fat dairy products. Fruit and vegetables are a major source of vitamins and minerals – we should eat at least five portions a day. As important as getting into healthy eating habits is eliminating bad ones, such as consuming too much salt, sugar, and alcohol.

LOW-FAT SNACKS
Regular snacks keep our energy levels up and may stop us overeating at mealtimes. Choose snack foods, such as fruit, that are low in fat, salt, and sugar. This helps to reduce the risk of heart disease and maintain a healthy weight.

Salmon provides healthy fats

Potatoes are rich in complex carbohydrate

Mangetout contain vitamin C

DIET AND EXERCISE
To maintain a healthy weight we need to balance the amount of food we eat with physical activity. A healthy weight helps prevent high blood pressure, heart disease, strokes, certain cancers, and the most common kind of diabetes. The more active we are, the more we can eat!

BALANCE YOUR PLATE
Healthy meals should contain a balance of nutrients. For example, this meal of grilled salmon served with mangetout and new potatoes provides a mix of high-quality protein (the salmon) as well as complex carbohydrates, fibre, vitamins, and minerals (the potatoes and mangetout). Eating balanced meals and small healthy snacks helps to keep blood glucose stable.

Fruit is an important part of a healthy balanced diet

Pasta is low in fat and a healthy way of filling up at mealtimes

Skimmed and semi-skimmed milk is healthier than full-fat milk

A VARIETY OF FOODS
Developing healthy eating habits is not difficult. In fact, choosing to eat a wide variety of foods makes things much easier. Most large supermarkets are laid out with the fresh fruit and vegetables, the dairy foods, the bread bakery, and the meat and fish counters on the outer sections of the shop. The inner aisles tend to be where the processed foods are found. Nutritionists encourage shoppers to fill their baskets with fresh foods first.

*Fresh fruit is rich
in nutrients such
as vitamin C*

*Add less salt to food
during cooking*

LESS IS BEST
A typical Western diet
contains far too much
sodium, which is linked
to high blood pressure.
Table salt is one source of
sodium, but 75 per cent
of the salt we eat comes
from processed foods.
Nutritionists advise
choosing reduced- and
low-salt versions of
processed foods.

CUT DOWN ON SUGAR
Sugar provides what nutritionists call
"empty calories" – calories without any
other nutrients such as vitamins or
minerals. Many people consume
unhealthy amounts of sugar.
Foods that are high in sugar,
such as cakes and biscuits, tend
also to be high in fat. When
choosing sweet snacks,
foods such as raisins are
healthier than sweets.

Stack of
sugar cubes

STICK TO ALCOHOL LIMITS
Several studies show that
people who drink alcohol in
moderation live longer than
those who are teetotal. More
recently, studies have shown
that one to two drinks a day
can reduce the risk of heart
disease by up to 30 per cent.
However, too much alcohol
can lead to serious health
problems. Certain types
of cancer, including liver
cancer, are more common
in heavy drinkers.

FRESH AND SEASONAL
The most nutrient-rich plant foods are those that are fresh,
seasonal, and harvested locally, rather than those that are
transported thousands of miles from the place in which they
are grown. Freshly picked fruit is rich in vitamins and healthy
substances known as phytochemicals. Even if we cannot pick
fruit straight from a tree, we can make sure that the foods we
buy are unprocessed or minimally processed. Highly processed
or convenience foods should be avoided where possible
because they often contain too much salt, sugar, and fat.

Carbohydrates

Lentils

COMPLEX CARBS
Lentils, rice, and beans are all excellent sources of starch, also known as complex carbohydrates (due to the number and arrangement of glucose units). They are a highly nutritious food source and form the basis of many dishes in different cultures all over the world.

Rice

OUR BODIES ARE POWERED by a major energy source known as carbohydrates. The basic unit of all carbohydrates is a substance called glucose. Some carbohydrates consist of long or complex chains of glucose units – these are called starches. Other carbohydrates contain very few glucose units – these are sugars. We get starches from plants, such as potatoes, grains, and beans, and sugars from foods such as honey, fruit, and milk, as well as from processed foods such as sweets, cakes, and biscuits. Whatever type of carbohydrate we eat, the body always breaks it down into glucose. This is the fuel that we burn to power the entire body from the muscles to the brain.

Beans

FIRST CROPS
Carbohydrates have formed the bulk of our diet since people first started farming carbohydrate-rich grain crops about 10,000 years ago. We know that the ancient Egyptians grew wheat and barley on the fertile banks of the River Nile. Once harvested, the grains were made into bread, soup, and beer.

Wholegrain bread

Wheat

Refined wheat products

OUR DAILY BREAD
Bread is a main source of carbohydrate made from wheat or other grains. If grain husks (the tough, outer parts) are left on when grain is ground into flour, the bread is wholegrain. Products such as croissants and white pitta bread are less nutritious because they contain refined flour – this means the husk is removed.

PASTA
Like bread, pasta is usually made from ground wheat. It is found in both wholegrain and refined forms, depending on how much of the husk is retained in the flour. Pasta comes in an enormous variety of shapes – from the thin strands of spaghetti to the seashell-shaped *conchiglioni*. Pasta is often combined with a meat or vegetable-based sauce to create a nutritious, carbohydrate-rich meal.

Starch grains

STARCH GRAINS

Starch exists in plants in the form of grains. The exact size and shape of the grains differ according to the plant. In its raw form starch is often indigestible, but when it is cooked, the grains swell and soften. This is why foods such as pasta, rice, and potato are difficult to eat when raw, but soft and edible after they have been boiled in water.

Magnified potato slice

Potatoes

SUGAR RUSH

The carbohydrates in chocolate and cola are sugars or simple carbohydrates. The body digests them quickly, which causes a rapid rise in the level of blood glucose – many nutritionists believe this to be unhealthy. This is one reason why it is sensible to limit sugary snacks in the diet.

Yam

Sweet potato

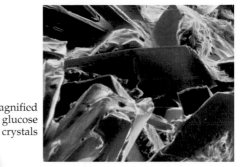

Magnified glucose crystals

DISCOVER YOUR ROOTS

Some plants store starch in the form of thickened underground organs called tubers. Potatoes, sweet potatoes, and yams are all examples of tubers. As well as being an excellent source of starch, they also contain vitamin C. The way tubers are cooked affects how quickly they release glucose into the body. For example, boiled potatoes release glucose at a medium rate, whereas baked potatoes release glucose quickly, giving us a fast burst of energy.

GLUCOSE STORES

After we eat a carbohydrate food, glucose enters our cells and is burned to produce energy. Our body can carry enough glucose to supply us with about an hour's worth of energy at a time. The excess is turned into a substance called glycogen, which is stored in the liver until it is needed.

EATING FOR ENDURANCE

Tour de France winner Lance Armstrong ensures that carbohydrates form 70 per cent of his diet. Eating large amounts of complex carbohydrates means that the body benefits from a gradual release of energy over time.

POTATO FAMINE

Over-reliance on potatoes for food and animal fodder resulted in a devastating famine for Irish peasants in 1845–49, when a disease known as blight caused potato crops to fail. Although carbohydrates should form a large part of our daily dietary intake, we should obtain them from a wide variety of plant foods.

Fibre

Dietary fibre is a large group of compounds that are found in plant foods such as beans, grains, and vegetables. Some types of fibre cannot be digested by enzymes in the digestive system and they pass through your body unchanged – but they still play an important role in a healthy diet. A high-fibre diet can help you control your weight because fibre fills you up and means that you have less room for fatty, high-calorie foods. In the late 1960s, scientists also uncovered a link between eating fibre and reducing the risk of chronic diseases. A high-fibre diet is particularly beneficial to the health of the intestines and is good for preventing constipation.

HIPPOCRATES
Although the word "fibre" has only been in use since the 1950s (your grandparents may still call it "roughage"), its dietary merits have long been debated. Hippocrates, the ancient Greek physician who is regarded as the father of medicine, recommended baking high-fibre bread as early as 430BCE for its beneficial effect on the intestinal tract.

HUNGRY HIPPOS
Grass-eating animals, such as the hippopotamus, have micro-organisms living in their digestive tract that can break down plant fibre into glucose (a type of sugar). Humans do not have these micro-organisms.

Lentils

Chickpeas

FIBRE-RICH FOODS
Different plant foods contain different kinds of fibre. The fibre in apples, for example, is different from the fibre in pasta. The amount of fibre present in a food also varies from plant to plant. The benefits of each type of fibre are different, too. That is why it is best to eat a variety of fibre-rich foods: wholegrains, cereals, fruit, vegetables, and legumes. You should aim to include 18g (0.6oz) of fibre in your diet every day.

Wholegrain cereal

Soluble fibre

Black-eyed peas

Insoluble fibre

INSOLUBLE AND SOLUBLE FIBRE
Fibre falls into two broad groups. Insoluble fibre acts like a sponge, expanding to hold water and increasing the bulk of the material that passes through your intestines. Soluble fibre lowers blood cholesterol, decreasing the risk of heart disease, and helps to control the level of blood glucose by slowing down the rate at which food leaves your stomach.

Wholemeal pasta contains more fibre than "white" pasta

Cellulose surrounds cell walls of plant

White bread contains 1.5g (0.05oz) of fibre per 100g (3.5oz)

WHOLE BREAD
Eating wholegrain products – breads, cereals, wholewheat pasta, and brown rice – is a good way to add fibre to your daily diet. But just because bread is brown does not mean it is high in fibre. Many products labelled "wheat bread" contain a mix of white and wholemeal flours, and so provide less fibre. Read nutrition labels carefully and look for the words "wholemeal", "wholegrain", or "wholewheat".

Eat apples unpeeled for the most fibre

WHY PLANTS CONTAIN FIBRE
Fibre helps to give plants their shape and structure. The most important type of structural fibre in plants is cellulose, which is constructed from long chains of glucose units. Cellulose surrounds cell walls giving them form and stability. The parts of plants that are rich in cellulose are the stalks, leaves, seeds, and grains.

Fresh cranberries

Wholemeal bread contains 5.8g (0.2oz) of fibre per 100g (3.5oz)

PECTIN-RICH FRUIT
Pectin is a form of soluble fibre that is found in fruits such as apples, cranberries, and citrus. (Pectin is also the substance that makes jam set.) Soluble fibre has been found to lower blood cholesterol levels. Fibre is concentrated in the skins and cores of fruit, so it is best not to peel them before eating.

Raw cabbage has more fibre than cooked

Broccoli stalks and florets are excellent sources of fibre

Good fats, bad fats

EATING TOO MUCH FAT can eventually lead to obesity and health problems, but in small amounts, fat is essential to the functioning of the body. Fats supply vitamins and essential fatty acids that the body cannot make itself, and also provide energy stores to draw upon when needed. Certain fats, for example, are crucial to a baby's developing brain and nervous system. Fats are substances derived from animal or plant sources and they come in both solid and liquid form. Most fats in your body and in foods are made up of molecules containing a varying number of hydrogen atoms. Exactly how many hydrogen atoms determines whether a fat is mostly "saturated" or "unsaturated". Saturated fats should only be eaten in moderation.

MARGARINE
Margarine, developed in France, was once hailed as a healthy alternative to butter. However, health experts now agree that the process by which some margarines are made – hydrogenation – creates an unhealthy type of fat that can raise cholesterol levels.

Fatty cuts of meat

Cakes and biscuits

SATURATED FATS
These fats are mostly solid at room temperature, and include most animal fats (butter, cheese, and fatty cuts of meat), as well as palm and coconut oils. A healthy diet limits saturated fats and hydrogenated fats, which are found in some margarines, cooking fats, and a wide range of biscuits, cakes, packaged baked goods, and fast food.

Butter

MONO-UNSATURATED FATS
Unsaturated fats may be either mono-unsaturated or poly-unsaturated. Mono-unsaturated fats are liquid at room temperature and have been found to lower cholesterol levels when they replace saturated fats in a diet. Good sources include olive, rapeseed, and ground nut oils, as well as avocado, and some nuts and seeds.

OIL AND WATER
All fats, whether liquid or solid, are insoluble. This means that they cannot be dissolved in water. To make products such as margarine and salad cream, which combine water with vegetable oil, substances known as emulsifiers must be added to prevent the oil and water from separating. Lecithin, derived from soya beans, is a commonly used emulsifier.

Olives are pressed to make olive oil

Fatty fish provide omega-3 fatty acids

Sunflower seeds

POLY-UNSATURATED FATS
Like mono-unsaturated fats, these fats are liquid at room temperature, and they either lower or have no effect on blood cholesterol levels. Poly-unsaturated fats are found in safflower, sunflower, corn, cottonseed, walnut, and soybean oils. Other sources include sunflower and sesame seeds, and nuts, such as almonds, pecans, and Brazil nuts. These fats help prevent blood clotting, which can trigger a stroke. They also help to lower the risk of heart disease.

ESSENTIAL FATTY ACIDS
Oily fish are an abundant source of essential fatty acids known as "omega-3s". These are important for building cell membranes, regulating blood pressure and clotting, and keeping the immune system healthy.

Sunflower oil

Sesame seeds

FAT-SOLUBLE VITAMINS
This is a micrograph of one of the acids that make up vitamin A. The only way to get the fat-soluble vitamins (A, D, E, and K) you need for good nutrition is to eat fat. Your body cannot make these vitamins by itself.

CLOGGED ARTERY
If the arteries become clogged with fatty deposits over a period of many years, this may restrict blood flow to the heart and increase the likelihood of having a heart attack.

Artery

Haemorrhage

Fatty deposit blocking artery

HOW FAT KEEPS US WARM
The fat that is stored underneath your skin acts like a blanket around the core of the body. This helps to insulate you and to prevent your temperature from dropping when you are in cold environments. Wearing thick or layered clothing, like this Inuit family, adds to this insulating barrier. People with little body fat are more likely to feel the cold than those with greater body fat.

Sumotori must use physical weight to prevent being pushed out of the ring

SUMO WRESTLERS
These men participate in the 2,000-year-old Japanese art of sumo. Their big bellies and strong, heavy legs lower their centre of gravity, making it hard to push them over. To achieve this shape, they eat huge quantities of a meat-rich stew called *chanko*. Because their calorie intake is so high they develop a large proportion of body fat. Sumo wrestling is one of the few physical activities where being overweight is an advantage – most sports require participants to be lean.

Mawashi
(sumo belt)

Salt is thrown across the ring as part of a pre-match ritual

Protein

WHICH CAME FIRST?
For many centuries, chickens have been farmed for their eggs, which are a valuable source of protein. One medium egg contains 7.2g (0.3oz) of protein, as well as B vitamins, vitamins A and D, zinc, and iron. Some people who do not eat meat choose to eat eggs, so that they obtain all the essential amino acids they need.

EVERY SINGLE CELL in the body needs protein for growth, maintenance, and repair. Proteins make up the antibodies that help shield you from disease, and the connective tissue that provides support throughout your body. You also need protein to make many enzymes and hormones, as well as the neurotransmitters that deliver messages to your brain. Protein is not a single substance, but a chain of chemicals called amino acids. Although protein is essential, you need relatively small amounts for good health. Just 10–15 per cent of your daily calories should come from protein.

FRANÇOIS MAGENDIE (1783–1855)
This French physiologist was the first person to observe that mammals cannot survive if deprived of dietary protein. He was also one of the first people to identify the three main nutrients (protein, carbohydrates, and fats).

Glutamic acid is an amino acid present in protein-rich plant foods

AMINO ACIDS
There are 22 different amino acids in the protein of the human body. Nine of these are "essential", meaning that they must be obtained from the foods you eat. The other 13 are "non-essential", meaning that you are able to manufacture them in your body from an excess of other amino acids.

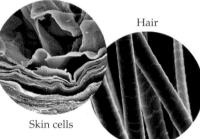

Hair

Skin cells

SUPPLE SKIN AND STRONG HAIR
Your body relies on protein to make skin, hair, and fingernails. The type of protein found in skin (and connective tissue) is collagen – it gives skin its thickness and suppleness. Keratin is the fibrous protein that gives hair and fingernails their strength and structure.

Methionine can be obtained from eggs

BUILDING UP MUSCLE POWER
Protein is the basic building material for muscle tissue. Body-builders need to consume higher amounts of protein than other people, because lifting weights creates tiny tears in the muscle that must be repaired. But eating a dozen eggs at a time is not enough. You need all-round, high-quality nutrition and proper strength training to build up your biceps.

Lysine is found in meat and fish

Building muscles is impossible without protein

COMPLETE PROTEINS

Essential amino acids cannot be created – you must get them from food. Foods containing all nine essential acids, including meat, fish, eggs, dairy products, and soya beans, are called "complete" proteins. "Incomplete" proteins, such as vegetables, grains, and beans, are low on, or are missing, certain amino acids.

Cheese provides a vegetarian source of protein

Egg whites are high in protein

Fish is an excellent source of protein and essential fatty acids

Beef contains about 20g (0.7oz) of protein per 100g (3.5oz)

Poultry is a good source of protein that is lower in fat than red meat

Vegetarian Indian *thali*

TOO MUCH PROTEIN?

Many people in developed countries, even vegetarians, regularly consume twice as much protein as they need. The body does not turn the excess into muscles, it stores it as fat, which can lead to health problems. In developing countries, it is the lack of protein that typically causes these problems.

Yoghurt adds dairy protein

PLANT SOURCES OF PROTEIN

You do not need to rely on animal products to get enough protein. Nuts, beans, grains, and vegetables all contain protein in varying amounts – and unlike some meats, they are low in saturated fats. Because different plant foods lack different amino acids, you must eat a variety of foods in combination to make sure you get all the essential amino acids.

Cooked lentils contain about 8g (0.3oz) of protein per 100g (3.5oz)

Green vegetables contain some protein

Potatoes contain about 2g (0.07oz) of protein per 100g (3.5oz)

Rice makes a complete protein when combined with lentils

White bread contains about 8g (0.3oz) of protein per 100g (3.5oz)

COMBINING PROTEINS

In many cuisines, people have combined plant-based protein foods to get complete proteins without knowing exactly why. Examples from across the globe include rice with lentils or beans, hummus with pitta, tofu with rice, and beans on toast.

Kidney beans contain about 22g (0.8oz) of protein per 100g (3.5oz)

Vitamins

LIMES TO PREVENT SCURVY
In the mid-1700s, Scottish naval surgeon James Lind discovered that drinking lime or lemon juice (rich in vitamin C) prevented scurvy. This disease was common among sailors due to poor diet on long voyages. Soon British ships never left port without limes, earning the sailors their nickname, "limeys".

WE NEED ONLY A FEW MILLIGRAMS of them a day, but vitamins are absolutely essential to good health. Vitamins are a group of 13 organic substances that our bodies need in order to work properly and to help regulate functions within cells. For the most part, we must obtain vitamins from the food we eat. Vitamins do not supply energy, but some of them help us to convert food to energy efficiently. Vitamins are grouped according to how they are absorbed and stored in the body. There are two groups: fat-soluble and water-soluble. Fat-soluble vitamins (A, D, E, and K) are stored in our fat tissues and liver. Water-soluble vitamins (the B vitamins and vitamin C) pass through the body quickly and must be replaced often.

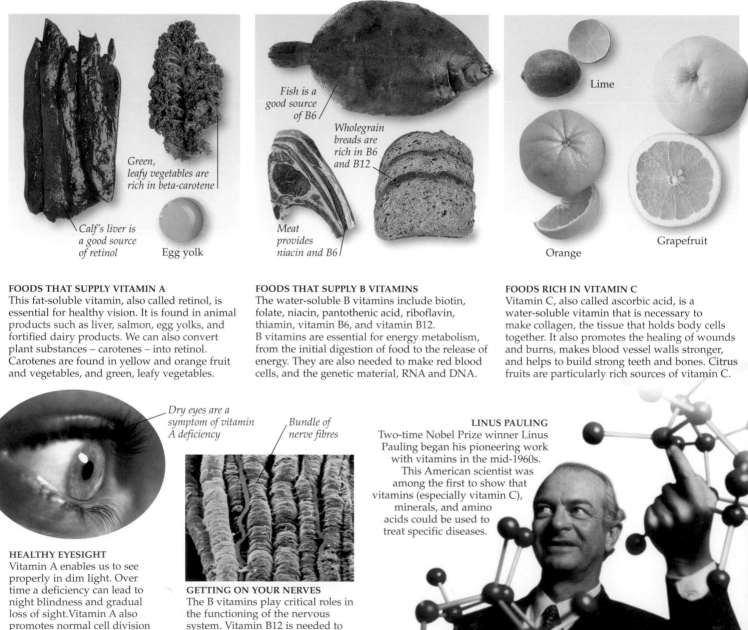

Green, leafy vegetables are rich in beta-carotene

Calf's liver is a good source of retinol

Egg yolk

Fish is a good source of B6

Wholegrain breads are rich in B6 and B12

Meat provides niacin and B6

Lime

Orange

Grapefruit

FOODS THAT SUPPLY VITAMIN A
This fat-soluble vitamin, also called retinol, is essential for healthy vision. It is found in animal products such as liver, salmon, egg yolks, and fortified dairy products. We can also convert plant substances – carotenes – into retinol. Carotenes are found in yellow and orange fruit and vegetables, and green, leafy vegetables.

FOODS THAT SUPPLY B VITAMINS
The water-soluble B vitamins include biotin, folate, niacin, pantothenic acid, riboflavin, thiamin, vitamin B6, and vitamin B12. B vitamins are essential for energy metabolism, from the initial digestion of food to the release of energy. They are also needed to make red blood cells, and the genetic material, RNA and DNA.

FOODS RICH IN VITAMIN C
Vitamin C, also called ascorbic acid, is a water-soluble vitamin that is necessary to make collagen, the tissue that holds body cells together. It also promotes the healing of wounds and burns, makes blood vessel walls stronger, and helps to build strong teeth and bones. Citrus fruits are particularly rich sources of vitamin C.

Dry eyes are a symptom of vitamin A deficiency

Bundle of nerve fibres

LINUS PAULING
Two-time Nobel Prize winner Linus Pauling began his pioneering work with vitamins in the mid-1960s. This American scientist was among the first to show that vitamins (especially vitamin C), minerals, and amino acids could be used to treat specific diseases.

HEALTHY EYESIGHT
Vitamin A enables us to see properly in dim light. Over time a deficiency can lead to night blindness and gradual loss of sight. Vitamin A also promotes normal cell division and growth, keeps skin, hair, and nails healthy, and helps to create strong bones and teeth.

GETTING ON YOUR NERVES
The B vitamins play critical roles in the functioning of the nervous system. Vitamin B12 is needed to make myelin (nerve fibres), while thiamine and B6 ensure that the nervous system works properly.

SOAKING UP THE SUNSHINE
We make vitamin D when our skin is exposed to ultra-violet (UV) rays from the sun. People who are not exposed to much sun, such as those who are housebound, need to get vitamin D from their diet.

Multi-vitamins are useful for those with a restricted diet

Vitamin C tablets are the most commonly taken vitamin supplement

Sunlight acts on a substance in the skin to create vitamin D

DIETARY SUPPLEMENTS
Millions of people take a vitamin tablet every day because they want to ensure they get all the vitamins they need. Research shows that most people could benefit from this, but no pill can replace a diet based around a variety of healthy foods.

Milk

Fortified cereals

Oily fish

Vegetable oils

Chicken

Nuts and seeds

Peas

Cabbage

FOODS THAT SUPPLY VITAMIN D
There are two forms of vitamin D. One is found in fortified cereals, egg yolks, oily fish, and fish-liver oils. The other is made by the body when exposed to the sun. Vitamin D is essential for calcium absorption (which is why it is sometimes added to calcium-rich dairy foods), and for building strong bones and teeth.

FOODS THAT SUPPLY VITAMIN E
This fat-soluble vitamin helps maintain healthy red blood cells and muscle tissue, protects fatty acids, and helps to prevent the destruction of vitamins A and D through oxidation (exposure to oxygen). Vitamin E is found in vegetable oils, eggs, mayonnaise, fortified cereals, and nuts and seeds, and in lesser amounts in chicken.

FOODS THAT SUPPLY VITAMIN K
This vitamin is needed for the normal clotting of the blood. About half of our vitamin K comes from our diet. It is widely available in cereals, and vegetables such as cabbage, spinach, peas, broccoli, and asparagus. The other half is manufactured by the bacteria that live in our intestines.

Alpha-tocopherol protects cell membranes from damage

VITAMIN E CRYSTALS
Vitamin E is a group of compounds, known as tocopherols, that share the same function. This micrograph shows the most potent vitamin E compound, alpha-tocopherol, which may help to protect us from heart disease.

VITAMIN K AT BIRTH
Because a deficiency in vitamin K can result in excessive bleeding from a very minor cut, many newborn infants are given a dose of this vitamin as a routine part of their post-natal care. This is because they may lack the intestinal bacteria needed to make the vitamin.

Child being given vitamin K in liquid form

Minerals

LIKE VITAMINS, MINERALS are only needed in very small amounts, but even in tiny quantities their presence is essential to good health. Minerals are vital to a number of processes in the body: bone and teeth formation, biological reactions, water balance, hormone production, and the functioning of the circulatory, nervous, and digestive systems. There are more than 60 minerals in the body, but only about 15 are considered essential, and we must ensure that these are present in the foods we eat. The best way to obtain enough minerals is to eat a varied and balanced diet based around fresh, minimally-processed foods. Getting too little or too much of a certain mineral can lead to health problems.

EARTH'S BOUNTY
Minerals are elements of the Earth's crust that are carried into ground water, soil, and sea by erosion. Plant roots take up some of these minerals. Humans and animals eating the plants absorb the minerals they contain.

BENDY BONES
Mineral deficiencies are linked to diseases. A lack of calcium can cause rickets, a painful condition in which the bones that support the body's weight soften and bend.

Rich in magnesium

Bananas

Provides potassium

Rich in phosphorus

Wholemeal bread

ESSENTIAL MINERALS
The eight essential minerals that we need in the greatest amounts are known as macrominerals. These are calcium, phosphorus, potassium, sodium, chloride, magnesium, iron, and zinc. The other seven essential minerals, of which we need less, are known as microminerals. These are fluoride, copper, selenium, iodine, manganese, chromium, and cobalt. All minerals interact with vitamins and other substances to maintain health.

Good source of zinc

Watercress

Egg

A GLASSFUL OF HEALTHY CALCIUM
Calcium is the most abundant mineral in the human body and builds our teeth and bones. This macromineral also helps to regulate heartbeat and other muscle contractions. Calcium is vital to young children, who renew their entire skeletons every two years. Dairy products, dark green leafy vegetables, nori seaweed, and tinned fish eaten with the bones are good sources of calcium.

TOO MUCH OF A GOOD THING?
Sodium is essential in small quantities to regulate blood pressure and water levels in the body. But many processed and convenience foods, from tinned soups to ready meals, are loaded with salt (sodium chloride). Eating too many sodium-rich foods can lead to high blood pressure and fluid retention, which strains the heart and kidneys.

FLUORIDE TOOTHPASTE
Toothpaste and tap water are our two main sources of the trace element fluoride. We need fluoride to help us build strong bones and teeth. Food sources include tea and seafood (especially if the bones are eaten).

Salt is raked into pyramid-shaped piles

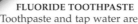

Pumpkin
seeds

Couscous
grains

Seaweed

Haemoglobin

Dried
apricots

Plain
chocolate

IRON-RICH VEGETARIAN FOODS
The iron found in meat and animal
products is better absorbed by the
body than the iron in plant foods.
This is why strict vegetarians
must ensure the foods they eat
are rich in iron. Grains, dried
fruit, leafy greens, seaweed,
nuts, seeds, and plain
chocolate are good sources
of iron. Eating a food
rich in vitamin C at the
same meal boosts iron
absorption further.

Nuts

RED BLOOD CELLS AND IRON
Iron is essential to the formation
of haemoglobin, a substance that
builds red blood cells (above) and
carries oxygen in the blood. Iron
also forms myoglobin, which
takes oxygen to muscle cells.
An iron deficiency affects the
body's ability to produce healthy
red blood cells and can lead to a
condition called anaemia.

Magnified limescale crystals

LIMESCALE DEPOSITS
Although minerals cannot be
destroyed, they can be lost
in the cooking process as
they dissolve in water. You
can see this clearly in a
kettle covered in limescale
(dissolved calcium). This
is why non-moist cooking
methods can help to
preserve the mineral
content of food.

SALT OF THE EARTH
The salt in your shaker was "harvested" from
the earth or sea. Rock, or mineral, salt is found
in solid deposits underground. It is mined and
brought to the surface for processing. The trace
mineral iodine, needed for cell metabolism, is
sometimes added to table salt during processing.
Salt can also be extracted from seawater in
shallow basins warmed by the sun (right).
The water evaporates into the air,
leaving the salt behind.

Healing foods

CHILLI PEPPERS
Not only do these colourful vegetables provide a spicy kick to many foods, chilli peppers are rich in phytochemicals. Capsaicin (the same substance that gives chillies their heat) is thought to be a powerful cancer fighter. Chillies are also rich in vitamin C.

Red chillis contain more beta-carotene

SINCE THE 1970s, SCIENTISTS HAVE FOUND that we can "borrow" certain natural defences when we eat plant foods. This is because plants are rich in natural compounds called phytochemicals, which defend against harmful bacteria, viruses, and cell damage. Phytochemicals also give plants their smell, colour, flavour, and texture. They work with nutrients and fibre to protect our bodies against disease, promote good health, and increase overall life expectancy. The best way to ensure we reap these benefits is to eat a variety of five to nine servings of fruit and vegetables every day. Antioxidants and "friendly bacteria", are other natural substances that are also found in food.

Free radical damage causes wrinkling of the skin

A healthy diet promotes young-looking skin

FREE RADICALS AND THE AGING PROCESS
Free radicals are substances produced by the body's normal metabolic processes. Over time, excess free radicals can cause damage to cells all over the body. They are responsible for the ageing of the body as well as for serious conditions such as cancer and heart disease. The way to neutralize the effect of free radicals is to eat plenty of foods that contain healing substances known as antioxidants.

Blueberries

Pomegranate

Juice sacs called arils

Lactobacillus is a friendly bacteria found in the gut

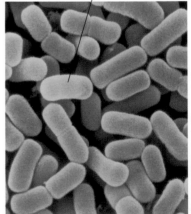

Sage, rosemary, and thyme are antioxidant herbs

ANTIOXIDANT FOODS
Many phytochemicals are also antioxidants. This means that they can fight the "oxidizing" damage done to the body by free radicals – think of it as the body rusting. Examples of antioxidants are anthocyanins in blueberries, polyphenols in pomegranates, and flavonoids in herbs such as rosemary and sage.

PINK PIGMENTS
Choosing to eat a colourful variety of foods is an easy way to get the benefits of phytochemicals. Plants and animals that are coloured orange, pink, red, and yellow – everything from carrots and oranges, to pink flamingos and salmon – contain carotenoids. These antioxidant pigments help the body to make vitamin A.

FRIENDLY BACTERIA
Billions of bacteria inhabit our digestive systems. Some are harmful, but others, called probiotic bacteria, are helpful. Maintaining a balance between the two is essential to good health. Eating foods that contain probiotic bacteria (fermented milk products and yoghurt) helps prevent the gut being colonized by harmful micro-organisms.

Garlic has been used as a remedy for everything from colds to the Black Death

GARLIC CLOVES

Since ancient times, people have believed that garlic gives strength and courage to those who ate it. The Egyptians ensured the pyramid builders ate plenty of garlic, and the Romans gave it to their army. In more recent times, researchers have found that garlic has important health benefits. Garlic contains allyl sulphides, which are natural antibiotics and powerful antifungals. They also help to lower unhealthy blood cholesterol, control blood pressure, and make blood less sticky and likely to form clots that could cause a heart attack or a stroke.

Uncooked garlic has most benefits

Lycopene is red pigment

POUR IT ON

Tomatoes contain a phytochemical known as lycopene that protects against heart disease and certain cancers. Processing food can destroy some phytochemicals, but in some cases makes them easier to absorb. For example, tomato ketchup contains more lycopene than raw tomatoes.

A HEALTHY BREW

This woman is harvesting tea leaves, which are dried and blended to make tea. Studies have shown that tea-drinkers enjoy several health benefits. Tea contains flavonoids: pigments that strengthen capillaries and other connective tissue, and protect against heart disease and certain types of cancer.

SUPER SOYA

Soya beans and soya products are rich in isoflavones, which may cut the risk of cancer and lower cholesterol. They can also help lower the risk of heart disease and osteoporosis (in which bones are prone to fracture). Choose soya milk, soya yoghurt, tofu, or edamame for the best health benefits.

Tofu is a low-fat protein

Linseed

Fennel

HEALTHY HORMONES

Plant foods such as fennel and linseed contain phyto-oestrogens that are similar to the female hormone oestrogen, though less potent. Including these foods in the diet may help to prevent breast cancer and lower the risk of heart disease. They are also beneficial after menopause.

Allergies and toxins

CAN YOUR DINNER BE DANGEROUS? Yes, if you have a severe food allergy. A food allergy is an abnormal immune system response to a food, such as peanuts or shellfish. Allergies often run in families and they tend to start in childhood. Fortunately, the number of people who have a true allergic reaction to foods (including symptoms such as gasping for breath, vomiting, or a skin rash) is fairly small. Much more common is a food intolerance in which people experience an undesirable reaction, such as bloating, after eating a particular food group, such as dairy products. There are also some foods that are naturally poisonous to everyone if they are not prepared or cooked in the correct way. These include red kidney beans, some species of mushroom, and a type of tropical fish.

RED KIDNEY BEANS
These beans contain lectin, a toxin that is common in many plants but is concentrated in high levels in red kidney beans. Eating raw or undercooked kidney beans can lead to extreme abdominal pain. It is important to cook them properly, to minimize possible exposure to the toxin.

MOREL MUSHROOMS
Morels are edible mushrooms that contain small amounts of a toxin called helvellic acid. Cooking morels destroys helvellic acid and makes them safe to eat – but they should not be eaten raw. A number of other mushrooms are also toxic, and some are similar in appearance to harmless mushrooms. Only eat mushrooms that you can correctly identify.

Citrus fruit

Chef has a special licence to prepare fugu

A DEADLY DELICACY
Fugu (a type of blowfish) is a delicacy in Japan, but it is also incredibly poisonous. The fugu's glands contain a toxin that is 270 times more toxic than cyanide. A specially trained chef works with a surgeon's skill to remove the glands without puncturing them. If this toxin is eaten, the diners have truly eaten their last meal!

Oysters

HISTAMINE CRYSTALS
British chemist George Barger (1878–1939) studied the role of the chemical histamine in allergic reactions. When someone with a food allergy is exposed to an allergen, histamine is released by the body (seen in the micrograph on the right) and this triggers an inflammatory reaction.

George Barger

WHO GETS FOOD ALLERGIES?
Babies are vulnerable to food allergies, so new foods are introduced to young mouths one at a time during weaning. There is also a three-day or longer wait between the introduction of each new food. This helps care-givers to identify which foods, if any, cause reactions. Many babies outgrow food allergies by the age of five, perhaps because their immune systems mature.

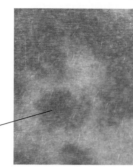

Skin rash from allergy

ALLERGY SYMPTOMS
Food allergy sufferers may experience a skin rash, abdominal pain, vomiting, diarrhoea, wheezing, itchy mouth, or runny nose. In extreme cases, a reaction known as anaphylactic shock occurs in which the throat swells and makes breathing difficult. This should be treated as a medical emergency.

WHAT IS A FOOD ALLERGY?
If you have a food allergy, your immune system responds to the offending food in your body by releasing antibodies. These stimulate cells to release histamine, which may cause inflammation in your digestive tract, skin, lungs, nose, and throat. The most common foods to cause allergies are shellfish (shrimp, crayfish, lobster, crab, mussels, and oysters), citrus fruit, peanuts and other nuts, wheat, milk, eggs, chocolate, and strawberries.

Peanuts

TESTING FOR FOOD ALLERGIES
If a patient's history indicates that a food allergy is likely, a doctor may give a scratch skin test (right). A dilute extract of the suspected food is placed on the skin of the forearm or back. This skin is scratched and observed for a reaction such as swelling. It is critical for anyone who has a food allergy to identify it and avoid the offending food.

Strawberries

FOOD INTOLERANCE
Coeliac disease (left) is an intolerance to gluten (found in wheat). A food intolerance can occur when the body fails to produce an enzyme needed for the digestion of a particular substance, such as lactose (sugar) in milk. Intolerances can also be a response to chemicals, such as caffeine, found in food or drink. Symptoms include gas and nausea.

Damaged intestinal walls in coeliac disease

Sorghum crop, Nebraska, US

Chocolate

EXCLUSION DIET
Allergies and intolerances can be managed by avoiding the "trigger" foods and finding alternatives. People who cannot tolerate wheat, for example, can eat cereals and bread based on sorghum, millet, and buckwheat instead. Exclusion diets can sometimes be challenging, especially for common "ingredient" foods such as milk and eggs.

Eggs

Digestion and absorption

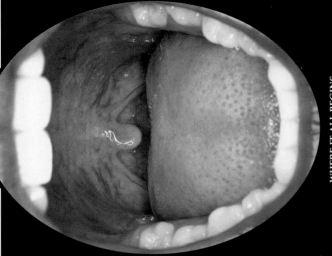

YOUR BODY CANNOT BENEFIT from the nutrients in food until they have passed through your digestive system and been absorbed into your cells and tissues. This process is known as digestion and absorption. Digestion takes place in a long tube known as the alimentary canal, which begins with your mouth and ends with your anus. In between the mouth and anus are your oesophagus, stomach, and small and large intestines. Each organ plays a key role in transporting or breaking down food, facilitating the absorption of nutrients, or removing waste from your body. Digestion is greatly speeded up by protein substances known as enzymes. Specific enzymes act on each of the major nutrients – carbohydrates, fats, and proteins – to break them down into their simplest components.

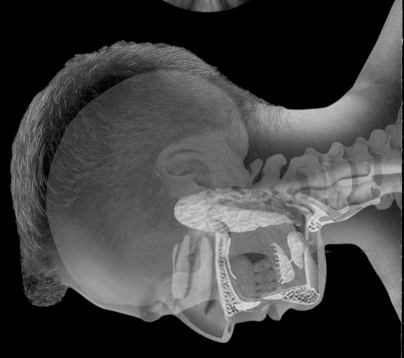

WHERE IT ALL BEGINS
The mouth is where digestion begins. Teeth tear and grind food into small pieces and salivary glands release an enzyme that starts breaking down carbohydrate. The tongue then moves balls of food to the back of the mouth ready to be swallowed.

Epiglottis seals off the larynx when you swallow

Epiglottis folds back when you are breathing

DOWN THE RIGHT PIPE?
When you swallow a bolus (ball of food) a flap of cartilage called the epiglottis folds back to cover your larynx, or voice box. This stops food from accidentally going down your trachea (windpipe). Swallowing is the last voluntary part of digestion. Next, the alimentary canal takes over.

WILLIAM BEAUMONT (1785–1853)
This American doctor treated a patient whose abdomen had been opened by a gunshot. The patient recovered, but his wound remained open, allowing Beaumont to discover the workings of the digestive system.

IVAN PAVLOV AND HIS DOGS
Russian scientist Pavlov (1849–1936) studied digestion in dogs to understand how some reflexes such as salivation can be manipulated. Dogs (like humans) salivate when they eat. Pavlov decided to ring a bell every time he fed his dogs. Soon, the dogs salivated in response to the bell, whether they were fed or not. But after several bell rings without food, the dogs no longer salivated at its sound.

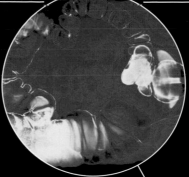

THE SMALL INTESTINE
After food has been in the stomach for about six hours, it is ready to enter the small intestine. Inside this narrow but long tube 5–6m (16–20ft) in length, food is bombarded with more enzymes from the pancreas and liver. Nutrients are absorbed into finger-like projections called villi (above) that line the walls of the small intestine.

THE LARGE INTESTINE
Next, food is squeezed into the large intestine (seen in the X-ray above). At about 1.5m (5ft) long, the large intestine is shorter and wider than the small intestine. Its function is to extract water and every last nutrient from food. Anything left over is prepared for expulsion through the urinary tract or the anus: the end of the line.

THE STORY OF DIGESTION
Digestion allows you to get the nutrients and energy you need from food. All the useable parts of food need to be made small enough and soluble enough to be absorbed by the cells and tissues of your body. Mechanical digestion, such as chewing teeth or a churning stomach, breaks food into smaller pieces. This makes it easier for digestive enzymes to carry out the process of chemical digestion.

THE STOMACH
Food and drink travel down the oesophagus to the next stop on the line: the stomach. The stomach is a stretchy, J-shaped bag of several strong muscle layers.
It breaks food down mechanically by churning it into mush. The stomach also breaks food down chemically by mixing it with enzymes. Mucus lining the stomach walls (above) stops it from digesting itself with these enzymes.

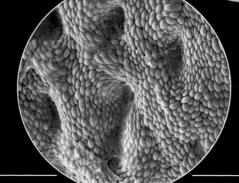

Dietary needs

EVERYONE NEEDS THE SAME nutrients for good health, but not everyone needs the same amounts of these nutrients. Nutrient and calorie needs vary from person to person, depending on factors such as age, sex, body size, the state of our general health, and our level of physical activity. Nutrition experts and scientists work together to analyse the current research on nutrition and to establish a set of guidelines called dietary reference values (DRVs). These DRVs tell us how much protein, carbohydrate, fat, vitamins, and minerals we need to eat every day. However, because we may eat more on some days than others, and tend to eat different foods from day to day, in practice, it is acceptable to average out our nutrient intake over several days.

HEALTHY SCHOOL DINNERS
Governments use DRV guidelines to set food policy. School dinners, for example, are based on DRVs. These dietary guidelines are also used by health professionals, the food industry, and organizations that create menus for hospitals, nursing homes, and prisons.

HOW MUCH DO WE NEED?
Nutritional needs change during a person's lifetime. In the first six months of life, for example, a baby grows and develops rapidly. Breast milk or infant formula milk meets all of a baby's requirements. But by six months, a shift in nutritional needs means that other foods must be introduced, during weaning. Nutritional needs continue to change throughout childhood. By age 11, boys have different nutritional needs from girls, a division that continues throughout adulthood.

A DIET THAT WORKS
Energy requirements depend in part on a person's lifestyle and activity levels. On average, boys have slightly higher energy needs starting from adolescence than girls. A manual labourer needs to consume more calories than a person in a sedentary job.

Recommended food and drink intake for an active man over one week

Bread provides B vitamins

Men aged 19–50 require 55.5g (2oz) protein every day

Shellfish is rich in protein

Grains are a source of carbohydrate

Vegetables provide vitamins and minerals

Recommended food and
drink intake for a baby
over one week

*Fresh fruit is
vitamin-rich*

*A one-year-old
baby needs about
15g (0.5oz)
protein a day*

SEE HOW THEY GROW
In the first three years of life, children need high
levels of energy because they are active and
growing rapidly. They also need high amounts
of almost all vitamins and minerals. They
should drink whole milk in preference to
skimmed. Young children should also
avoid eating too many high-fibre foods,
which are filling and can leave little
space for more valuable nutrients.

*Whole milk
has high fat
content –
important for
babies and
children*

*Bread provides
carbohydrate*

*Cereals may be
fortified with
vitamins and
minerals*

*Cheese is a
good source
of calcium*

*Peas are
nutritious and
easy to digest*

*Babies enjoy chewing
carrot sticks*

*Fish provides
protein*

*Eating healthy
vitamin- and
mineral-rich
snacks is
important
during
pregnancy*

EATING FOR TWO
In pregnancy, there is an increased
need for some (but not all)
nutrients. Women planning a
pregnancy must get an
adequate amount of folate, a
vitamin found in pulses and
green vegetables. This helps to
reduce the risk of defects in the
unborn child.

*Older
people can
stay fit and
active by
eating
healthily*

GOLDEN YEARS
After the age of 50 in women and 60
in men, energy requirements begin to
decrease gradually. Because older
people still need the recommended
amounts of vitamins and minerals
from less calories, they may need to
take dietary supplements.

CHECKING FOOD LABELS
Because DRVs were developed mainly for
health professionals rather than individuals,
it is difficult to base a diet around them. The
nutritional labels found on food products
contain a simpler form of the DRVs that
is much easier for consumers to
understand. Food labels provide an at-
a-glance guide to the nutritional and
energy values per serving.

NUTRITION IN A BOTTLE
Some food and drink
manufacturers add extra
vitamins and minerals to
products such as fruit juice
and mineral water. This
can help us to reach our
daily requirements of
nutrients, such as calcium,
without consuming too
many calories.

Mineral water

*Kidney stones
in X-ray*

EVERYTHING IN MODERATION
Some nutrients are toxic when consumed
in excess. Although rare, an excess of
vitamin D can lead to kidney stones –
hardened crystal deposits that form in the
urinary system. DRVs include guidelines about
the maximum amount we should eat of a nutrient.

Making food last

NOTHING LASTS FOR EVER, and that includes food. Methods for keeping food edible date back thousands of years – the ancient Romans rubbed salt on meat to dry it out, just as we cure pork today. When fresh foods are scarce, preserving food is vital for survival. There are several methods of food preservation. Harmful micro-organisms do not survive at extreme temperatures, or where moisture has been removed, so heating, freezing, drying, or the addition of preservatives are all ways in which food can be kept safe and tasty to eat for months, and even years.

Italian prosciutto ham is cured for up to 18 months

DRY CURING
Meat and fish can be preserved by dry curing – rubbing salt on them, and hanging them to dry for months. This removes moisture and kills bacteria. As the air circulates around the meat, such as this Italian prosciutto ham, it forms a crust on the outside that keeps the inside tender. This crust is later removed and discarded.

SMOKE 'EM OUT
Once meats or fish have been cured, they can be smoked over the smouldering embers of a fire. Practised since prehistoric times to speed up the drying process, smoking is now used to enhance a food's flavour, colour, and aroma.

Herrings hung out to dry in the open air

HUNG OUT TO DRY
Hanging food to dry in the sun is another ancient method of food preservation. The wind and heat remove the moisture that allows bacteria to breed. The length of time that food takes to dry depends upon its type and thickness. If heat is applied too quickly, the outside becomes cracked and the inside remains moist, which can lead to mould developing inside.

Pickles in airtight jars

A CANNY INVENTION
In the early 1800s, the French emperor Napoleon offered a prize to anyone who could invent a way to preserve military food supplies. A chef named Nicolas Appert devised a sterilization method in which jars of food were heated to kill bacteria. By 1880, manufacturers were producing food in metal cans similar to those of today.

Nicolas Appert
(1749–1841)

IN A PICKLE
Pickling dates back an incredible 4,000 years. The Egyptian queen Cleopatra attributed some of her beauty to eating pickles. In pickling, a wide variety of foods, such as vegetables and fish, are placed in jars and covered in a solution with a high acid content, such as vinegar. The acidity of vinegar prevents harmful micro-organisms from growing inside the jars, and preserves the food.

Food is poured
or squeezed
into the can

Food is heated at
high temperature
to destroy
micro-organisms

Astronauts'
meals

DEHYDRATED FOOD
Food can be made light
and long-lasting by a process
known as "lyophilization". In a
vacuum (conditions under which
the air is removed), liquid stored inside the
food turns into vapour (gas) without passing
through a liquid stage first. Freeze-dried coffee
is a good example of this preservation method.

IT'S IN THE CAN
Bottling and canning work on the same principles. Food is
sterilized by heating and, because there is no air in the can,
the food stays sterile until the can is opened. Cans are widely
used because they are robust and cheap to make. The food
inside can be heated to 120°C (250°F), which can kill
potentially deadly bacteria. Each food requires a different
heating time to ensure food
safety while preserving
taste and nutrients.

Micrograph
of benzoic
acid

ADDITIVES THAT PRESERVE FOOD
Since the advent of processed foods in the second half
of the 20th century, natural and artificial additives
that preserve foods have been widely used by
manufacturers. This is benzoic acid – otherwise
known as E210 – a crystalline substance used as a
food preservative. It restricts the growth of
moulds, fungi, yeast, and some bacteria.

Cooking food

COOKING IS THE PROCESS OF HEATING FOOD prior to consumption. For thousands of years, early people ate everything raw. So why do we cook? Heat kills harmful parasites and micro-organisms, and breaks down tough meat and plant fibres, making them easier to chew and digest. Cooking makes food look, smell, and taste better, too – the physical and chemical changes create all kinds of different flavours, textures, aromas, and colours. Cooking methods fall into two categories: dry-heat methods, which include baking, grilling, and frying, and moist-heat methods, which include simmering, stewing, and boiling. Some methods are considered healthier than others. For example, steaming is preferable to frying because it preserves vitamins and does not add fat to food.

COOKING WITH FIRE
Prehistoric people "tamed" fire about 500,000 years ago, but no-one knows when or why people first used it for cooking. Some speculate that cooking was discovered by accident – for example, an animal carcass was left too close to the fire. Because cooking softens food and makes it more edible, the young and the old had a better chance of survival by eating cooked food.

EARLY COOKING METHODS
The earliest method of cooking was probably roasting food over a fire. Food may also have been steamed by wrapping it in wet leaves and burying it in the embers, or cooked in hollow rocks or skulls. Clay pot cooking (above) originated sometime after 6000BCE.

THE THRILL OF THE GRILL
The delicious smells and the sizzle and pop of foods cooked under or over flames is just as appealing now as it may have been to early people. Grilling involves cooking food quickly at a high temperature. Food exposed to direct heat develops a crust on its exterior while the insides stay moist. Grilling is considered a healthy method of cooking fatty foods, such as meat, because the fat is allowed to drip off as the food cooks.

Stir-fry vegetables stay crisp

Boiling makes vegetables tender

COOKING FOOD IN LIQUID

Moist-heat cooking is a good method to preserve the flavour of delicate foods. In about 500BCE, it was done by digging a pit in the ground, lining it with stones, filling it with water, and tossing in hot rocks from the fire to make the water bubble and cook the food. Now we can set a pan of food in liquid on a gas or electric stove.

The first microwaves were huge, and expensive

FAST FOOD

The first microwave ovens were introduced in 1947. Ads for this Radarange model boasted that chicken pieces could be cooked in just three minutes. By the 1980s, microwave ovens were widespread. During microwaving, food is bombarded with electromagnetic waves that heat the water molecules.

COOKING WITH FAT

Fat can be heated to a high temperature so that it cooks food quickly and seals in flavour and moisture. There are several techniques for cooking with fat. Frying involves heating food in a pan covered with a film of fat. Deep-fat frying means immersing food in hot fat. Stir-fried food is stirred and tossed very quickly in a pan or wok using a minimal amount of oil.

HEARTH AND HOME

In wealthy households such as this 19th-century French home, kitchens were the domain of servants. But for many people throughout history, the kitchen was not a room in a house – it was the house. People lived in one room around a fire, used for cooking, warmth and light. Later, the kitchen became a separate room.

CONTEMPORARY KITCHENS

Modern kitchens are not just functional, but are as sleek and stylish as any other room in the house. Time-saving appliances and a trend towards "convenience" foods mean that cooks spend less time slaving over a hot stove.

Cuisine

THE COOKING TRADITIONS, practices, and food and beverages associated with a particular region are called its cuisine (from the French word for kitchen). For thousands of years, cuisine was influenced by food availability. People ate whichever animals they could catch and whatever fruits and vegetables grew near them. Religious food laws also played an important role in the development of a region's cuisine. In the last century, improvements in food distribution brought the world's cuisines into contact with each other. Many people now have access to dishes from other parts of the globe as well as their own regional cuisines.

LOCAL FOODS, REGIONAL CUISINE
This medieval picture shows people picking olives for cooking. In the past, eating food that was grown or reared locally was most people's only option. Today, there is renewed interest in local, seasonal food because it is fresh and environmentally friendly, in that it does not have to be transported huge distances by air or land.

COOKING BY THE BOOK
This Italian cookery book was published in Venice in 1622. Cookery books set out the cuisine of a nation or region, through recipes and instructions for cooking techniques. The oldest-known cookery book may be *Of Culinary Matters* by Roman Marcus Apicius, written in the first century.

Chillies add heat

Singapore: rice noodles, chinese sausage, and seafood

Gravy is traditionally made using the meat juices

Alsace, France: sauerkraut with potatoes and meat

FOODS OF THE WORLD
Diets vary throughout the world, but many cuisines feature a starchy food (for example, rice, yams, cassava, pasta, or bread) served with vegetables and meat or fish. Some foods, such as kebabs, noodles, and dumplings, are found in slightly different forms in many cuisines of the world.

Great Britain: roast beef and Yorkshire pudding

Edible species of water lily

South Africa: water lily and lamb stew

Southern USA: ribs, cornbread, greens, and black-eyed peas

Middle East: lamb kebabs and couscous

China: Wonton soup

EATING OUT
Restaurants are places where we can eat dishes from a specific cuisine or a mixture of cuisines (such as Tex-Mex). Diners may also observe the customs that are linked to a cuisine, such as eating with chopsticks in a Chinese restaurant. Before restaurants were established in the 1700s, street vendors, inns, and taverns sold local cuisine to the public.

GLOBALIZATION OF CUISINE

Improvements in food production, preservation, and transportation have made the world's cuisines more accessible to all. But there are fears that exporting some cuisines (for example, fast food) will also "export" the health risks that may be associated with them, such as obesity and heart disease.

A chef's hat is called a toque

THE RISE OF THE CHEF

A chef (from the French word for "chief") helps to preserve, promote, develop, and re-invent traditional cuisines. The chef truly is the chief in the kitchen – duties include recipe and menu creation, cooking, and overseeing a staff of cooks and pastry chefs. Since the 1980s, many chefs have become media stars, with their own television shows, food lines, and restaurants.

AUGUSTE ESCOFFIER (1846–1935)

This celebrated French chef was known as the "king of chefs and the chef of kings". His cooking made him famous the world over. In addition, Escoffier wrote several cookery books that captured the art of French cuisine. These are now regarded as classics.

Stuffed snails

Frog

ACQUIRED TASTES

Some foods that are considered delicacies in one country's cuisine, such as snails and frogs' legs in France, are reviled in others. A taste for such foods is usually acquired over time. For example, the durian, a large, spiky oval-shaped fruit native to Malaysia, may not appeal at first. The smell of durian has been compared to that of sewage!

Food and culture

THE FOOD WE EAT says a lot about who we are. But how, where, and when we eat, as well as who we eat with, are also part of our identity. Food historians study food and eating habits as way of learning about culture in general. The foods we choose help us to identify ourselves as individuals, as family members, as citizens of a nation, and as members of an ethnic population. Our food choices and preferences can mark differences between us, but food can also bring people together, strengthening cultural bonds.

Japanese chopsticks

CULTURAL EXPORTS
With the rise of globalization, food is now one of the major ways a culture "exports" itself. Food customs (such as the Far East practice of eating with chopsticks), as well as regional cuisines, are exchanged.

STATE DINNER
Sharing foods helps to mark an alliance between cultures. Throughout history, visiting heads of state have been honoured with elaborate banquets, often featuring the best of a nation's cuisine. In this medieval painting, a Portuguese king entertains a British monarch.

Sheep's eye

UNUSUAL FOODS
Cultures vary in terms of the foods that are considered acceptable. For example, boiled sheep's eyes are a delicacy in the Middle East. Deep-fried insects are regarded as a healthy protein-rich snack in some Asian countries.

Fried crickets, Cambodia

AROUND THE TABLE
Preparing and sharing food together is an important family activity all over the world. Mealtimes provide a valuable opportunity to socialize. However, in some Western countries the habit of eating as a family is in decline. This may be due to the pressures of work or the availability of easily prepared ready meals, which allow people to eat whenever they like.

Yams are a starchy type of vegetable

Turkey is the centrepiece of the meal

FEAST DAY
The ritual eating of certain foods for holiday meals is an important cultural event. The traditional foods eaten at an American Thanksgiving – for example, roast turkey, cornbread stuffing, pumpkin, and cranberries – are native to the New World, rather than the original homes of the celebrants.

CELEBRATING THE HARVEST
Food and drink harvest festivals, celebrated by nearly all cultures across the globe, help people to preserve and protect their culture. In the case of Milamala, the yam festival celebrated by the Trobrian Islanders in Papua New Guinea (above), the festival also encourages villagers to grow more yams so that everyone has enough to eat.

FOOD AND NATIONAL IDENTITY

Food plays a strong role in establishing a national identity. The Japanese tea ceremony, for example, is a ritual that evolved sometime in the 1200s and is still treasured today. In the tea ceremony, honoured guests share a communal bowl of green tea, as well as a meal or sweet snack. Each step in the ceremony is performed in a set order. A tea ceremony can last anywhere from one to five hours.

Multi-layered wedding cakes date from the 1850s

Hostess wears a kimono

FOOD AND SOCIAL CLASS

Food is a symbol of wealth. The kind of food a person eats tells other people something about his or her social status. In this painting, *The Crumbs from the Rich Man's Table*, the remains of a banquet are handed out to the poor in London.

FOOD AND CELEBRATION

Food is an important part of many celebrations across the world. One of the foods commonly associated with celebration is also one of the simplest: bread. The first wedding cake (in Roman times) was a bread loaf broken over the bride's head for good luck. Sharing the crumbs was also considered lucky.

Ceramic container for tea powder

Food and belief

ALTHOUGH MOST NUTRITIONISTS recommend that we eat a wide variety of foods, many people around the world choose to restrict their diets. The majority of these people are following religious dietary laws. These laws may prohibit certain foods completely, as well as set down restrictions about how various types of food must be prepared or cooked. Other people choose to limit what they eat for personal reasons. For example, vegetarians exclude animal flesh from their diet because they believe that killing animals is wrong or because they believe that a vegetarian diet is better for their health.

HALAL MEAT
This butcher in Cairo, Egypt, sells halal meat, meaning that the animals have been slaughtered following strict Islamic rules. Animals must be killed by cutting their throats to allow the removal of all blood from the carcass.

Bread is unleavened because there was no time to bake before fleeing

Bitter lettuce symbolizes the Jews' plight

Egg is a sign of spring

Meat on the bone is a sign of sacrifice

LAMB FOR EASTER
Many religious holidays have powerful associations with certain foods. For example, Jewish families may eat lamb at the spring holiday of Passover, to remember the lambs sacrificed at the first Passover. Many Christians serve lamb at Easter time because lamb has come to represent Christ's sacrifice.

CEREMONIAL MEALS
Judaism sets out its dietary laws (called "kashrut", or "keeping kosher") in the Torah, the holy book. These rules forbid certain foods and instruct cooks to keep meat and dairy produce separate. The Jewish holiday of Passover is marked with a special meal called the "seder" (right). Each food served is symbolic, to remind celebrants of the exodus of Jewish people from slavery in ancient Egypt.

Parsley is salty, like slaves' tears

Horseradish is as bitter as slavery

Walnut and apple mix is like the mortar used by brick-laying slaves

Unleavened wafer

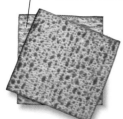

Chalice of wine

Cakes to celebrate the end of Ramadan

Muslims pray at a mosque

THE SACRAMENT
Members of the Catholic, Anglican, Eastern Orthodox, and many Protestant faiths share a ceremony of thankfulness known as the sacrament (or communion). While each denomination has its own specific beliefs and practices, in general, celebrants drink a sip of wine to represent the blood of Jesus Christ, and eat a wafer of unleavened (yeast-free) bread to represent the body of Christ.

A MONTH OF FASTING
In the ninth month of the Islamic calendar, followers of the Islamic faith observe a period of fasting known as Ramadan. During this month, Muslims go without food from dawn until sunset. After sunset, they break their fast with a snack, and a light meal after evening prayers. At the end of Ramadan, Muslims celebrate with a three-day feast.

WHAT IS VEGETARIANISM?

Removing some or all animal products from the diet is known as vegetarianism. People practice vegetarianism in several different ways. Vegans avoid all animal products. Ovo-lactovegetarians eat eggs and milk products, and lacto-vegetarians eat milk products, but not eggs. Fruitarians eat mainly fruits and berries.

Vegetables are rich in vitamins and minerals

Olive oil is an alternative to animal fat

Fruit may be eaten in all types of vegetarian diets

Legumes and pulses for protein

AN ANCIENT VEGETARIAN

Greek philosopher and mathematician Pythagoras (c. 580–500BCE) advocated a strict vegetarian diet in his writings. He believed that it was immoral to kill living creatures and sacrifice an animal's life simply for human nourishment. Until the 1800s, vegetarianism was known as the Pythagorean diet.

MACROBIOTIC DIET

Based on ancient Far Eastern principles of balance and harmony, a macrobiotic diet emphasizes fresh, seasonal wholefoods (usually vegetarian) combined into meals. Wholegrains, vegetables, and miso (a fermented soya soup, left) make up about three quarters of the macrobiotic diet, while protein, seaweeds, fruits, seeds, nuts, and drinks are added sparingly.

VEGETARIANISM AND RELIGIOUS BELIEF

Across the globe, the majority of people who follow a vegetarian diet do so for religious reasons. Many religions (Buddhism, Hinduism, Taoism, and especially Jainism) advocate a vegetarian diet, although it is not always compulsory. Many members of these faiths feel that all life should be valued, and anything obtained at the expense of animal suffering must be forbidden.

Buddhist monks in Cambodia

Attitudes towards food

CHEAP AND READY TO EAT – this is what today's consumers seem to demand from food. Globalization, technology, and marketing have combined to change our attitudes towards food dramatically in recent decades. But at what cost? Many are concerned that the multi-billion pound food industry prioritizes consumer demand over food safety and the health of the environment. And, like any other big business, the food industry uses advertising to influence our attitudes. Many ads for fast food are targeted directly at young children. Other concerns about modern eating patterns centre around the quantity of calories that we consume. Diet books often top the bestseller lists, yet obesity and eating disorders are on the rise.

FAST FOOD
These freshly cooked doughnuts may make your mouth water, but a look at recent fast food statistics is enough to make your jaw drop. In 2004, UK consumers spent £10 billion on fast foods such as burgers, fried chicken, and chips. In the US, the figure is $113 billion. Fast food is the largest sector of the food market.

FOOD MILES
Because consumers demand food that is both cheap and varied, food now travels increasing distances from the place where it is produced to the place where it is eaten. We refer to these distances as "food miles". There is an growing environmental cost associated with food miles – for example, the petrol burned by this lorry hauling fruit.

READY WHEN YOU ARE
There is a rising demand across the globe for pre-packed ready meals that can be heated and eaten quickly. These foods are heavily processed and may contain high levels of salt, fat, and additives. If they are eaten regularly, they can lead to weight gain and health problems in the long term.

Larger-than-life characters are used to market food

FOOD ADVERTISING
Children are drawn to foods promoted by colourful cartoon characters or famous names in sport or music – and food manufacturers know it. They routinely appeal to children with advertisements for foods that contain unhealthy levels of fat, salt, and sugar. Many governments are considering a ban on advertising to children.

COUCH POTATO CRISPS
Recent studies have shown that the proportion of overweight or obese children is skyrocketing in the West. This is a public health time bomb, as overweight children may go on to become overweight adults. Obese adults are at risk for a range of health problems, including diabetes and heart disease.

EATING DISORDERS
An eating disorder occurs when mental health issues affect normal eating. Anorexia nervosa (right) is voluntary starvation leading to extreme weight loss. Bulimia is characterized by episodes of binge eating followed by vomiting. The latest eating disorder to be diagnosed is orthorexia nervosa (an obsession with healthy eating).

The model "Twiggy" in the 1960s

Renoir nude, 1912

WHO'S THE FAIREST OF THEM ALL?
The body shape idealized by society changes over time. Plumpness was once seen as a symbol of beauty, whereas today in the West, the opposite is true. There is now concern that young people are under too much pressure to be thin.

Dr Atkins first published his Diet Revolution *in 1972*

The Atkins diet emphasizes protein and fat

CELEBRITY CHEFS
Cookery programmes were once hidden in television schedules. Now, to cater to the huge interest in home cuisine and fresh ingredients, food shows have become prime-time viewing. Many chefs, such as Jamie Oliver (left), are household names. Celebrity chefs not only create recipes but also open restaurants, write cookery books, and endorse products.

DIET FADS
Diet fads come and go and then come back again. In the 1970s, American doctor Robert Atkins proposed a high-protein, high-fat, low-carbohydrate diet that went against nutritional guidelines. The diet fell out of vogue but has recently become popular again as a way of losing weight.

Crop staples

AGRICULTURE IS THE PROCESS of producing food and other products by cultivating plants and raising domestic animals. Early people lived nomadic lives, but as agriculture developed, people settled in one place and stayed there with their crops. As farming began to support a greater number of people, communities began to grow. Today, farmers in developing countries might produce just enough food for themselves and their families, but in many parts of the world crop farming is big business, and, assisted by developments in science and technology, it takes place on a huge scale.

WORKING FOR LANDOWNERS
Medieval peasants are shown here tilling the soil surrounding the landowner's castle. Struggles between wealthy landowners and their poor, landless labourers have been a feature of farming through the ages. Inequality in wealth has always been a divisive issue – from the peasant's revolts of the Middle Ages to the struggle of landless people in developing nations today.

AT THE PLOUGH
In early history, agriculture probably developed and disappeared a few times before people began settling down in permanent farming communities. Each time a new farm implement, such as a hoe or a plough (above), was invented or improved, it profoundly changed farmers' lives.

Potatoes

Rice   Maize

MAJOR CROPS
Over many centuries, humans have selected a small number of plants to grow as food. There are more than 300,000 species of plant, but an estimated 95 per cent of human food comes from just 30 of these, eight of which are cereal grains. Today, the leading food crops grown worldwide are wheat, rice, maize, and potatoes.

Wheat

MECHANICAL INVENTIONS
Until the late 1800s, sowing, cultivating, and harvesting crops were done by hand (and still are in developing nations), with oxen and horses providing pulling power. Since that time, mechanical inventions from the reaper to the combine harvester have taken the toil out of farming. They have also increased farm efficiency and productivity. In 1830, it took about 300 hours of labour to produce 100 bushels of wheat. A modern farmer can do that in just three hours.

WATERING THE PLANTS
The process of supplying water to crops planted in dry places is called irrigation. Many irrigation methods, such as digging ditches to divert water (in Sudan, left) have been practised since farming began. Other crop irrigation methods include channelling water through pipes, using sprinklers, or deliberately flooding the land.

PLANTING RICE
These Japanese farmers are planting rice in flooded fields. Rice is a grass plant that feeds more than half of the world's population and is grown on every continent except Antarctica. In some languages, the word for "eat" means "eat rice".

THE BLUE CORN DANCE
Here, Native Americans are performing in the Blue Corn Dance, a Pueblo dance to celebrate the growing cycle of corn. Throughout history, people of many cultures have gathered to pray or give thanks for a bountiful harvest. The ancient Greeks paid tribute to Demeter, the goddess of grain, while the Romans made offerings to Cereas, the goddess of corn (and the root of the word "cereal").

Beer

Flatbread

GRAIN PRODUCTS
Grains provide about 50 per cent of the world's calories in a diverse range of foods. Wheat, for example, may be made into many different types of bread and pasta, as well as couscous, bulgur (cracked wheat), semolina, and beer.

Pasta

Livestock

Rooster

HUMANS BEGAN DOMESTICATING animals about 10,000 years ago. They raised them for meat or to harvest animal products, such as milk, eggs, and wool. As with the spread of crop farming, this practice brought about profound changes in society. Simple hunter-gatherer tribes settled down to form more complex societies, and populations exploded because of the improved nutrition that animal foods provided. Animals also supplied labour (by pulling heavy loads), fuel and fertilizer (in the form of manure), transportation, and clothing. Today, livestock farming is a vast global enterprise.

ANIMAL FARMING
Livestock farming may have begun when early farmers tried to control wild creatures that nibbled crops. The beneficial side effect of taming animals was an easily available meat supply. The animals that were most easily domesticated were those with a flexible diet, a non-aggressive temperament, and the ability to breed in captivity.

COCK-A-DOODLE-DOO
Chickens are the most common birds on Earth, with an estimated global population of 24 billion. These creatures probably evolved from an Asian jungle bird. They became valuable to farmers for their meat, as well as their eggs and alarm calls. By 4000BCE the Chinese ate chicken and eggs in a variety of ways. Egyptians and Romans were also partial to chicken dishes.

PINK PORKERS
A native of Europe, the Middle East, and parts of Asia, the pig was domesticated about 6,000 years ago. Pigs are raised mainly for their meat (pork). An old saying maintains that there is a use for every part of a pig apart from its squeal. Their skins are used to make leather and their bristly hairs make paintbrushes.

Highland cow

Aberdeen Angus

BREEDS OF CATTLE
All domestic cattle are descended from an animal known as an aurochs – to which the Highland cow is most similar in appearance. Cattle have been valuable throughout history for their meat (beef) and dairy foods, as well as for farm labour. Cattle are sometimes regarded as the oldest form of wealth.

Hereford bull

ON THE HOOF
Livestock is the world's largest land user, and the worldwide demand for meat is growing. According to the United Nations Food and Agricultural Agency, livestock contributes to the livelihoods of 70 per cent of the rural poor. But large-scale livestock production may put the environment at risk. Herds like this one in California compact the soil, making it less suitable for crops. Wastes contribute to surface and groundwater pollution.

THE DEMAND FOR MEAT

Population growth and increasing affluence are just two of the factors that have led to a greater demand for meat. Yet concerns about the spread of animal diseases to humans has also increased.

FEEDING LIVESTOCK

On the farm, animals provide a source of labour and raw materials for clothing (such as sheep's wool) as well as food. But animals need to eat and drink, too. A farmer must set aside land to grow grains for livestock to consume that otherwise would have been used for human crops. In addition, animal waste must be managed safely.

ANIMAL SCIENCES

The science of breeding and raising livestock is known as animal husbandry. While little is known about its early development, selective breeding of livestock was practised as far back as Roman times. Today, people who study animal science may go on to become a vet, like this man, right.

UNUSUAL LIVESTOCK

In many countries, the demand for exotic meats has skyrocketed as people search for novel low-fat, high-quality protein sources. Some farmers have profited from raising unusual livestock. New faces down on the farm include ostrich (right), buffalo, elk, and llama.

Dairy foods

DOOR-TO-DOOR DELIVERY
Modern dairying began in the late 1800s, as more people moved to cities from rural areas. In this 1902 photograph, milk churns are loaded on to a horse-drawn cart. The cart went from house to house, and people filled their own jugs from the churns.

Dairy farming is the industry of raising female cows for the production of milk and milk products such as cheese and butter. Dairy farms tend to be found where there is an abundant water supply (milk is 87 per cent water) and inexpensive farmland. It is thought that people began milking cows in about 3000BCE. From about 1850, the invention of specialized dairy machines and advances in food technology helped to modernize dairy farms and increase milk production. Milk is valued as a complete food containing nearly all of the nutrients that we need for health – this is why milk is an an important part of a child's diet.

LOUIS PASTEUR (1822–1895)
This French chemist pioneered the technique of pasteurization – heating food in order to kill harmful micro-organisms. Most commercially available dairy products are now pasteurized. This extends their shelf life and makes them safer to eat without significantly affecting their nutritional value.

Goat's milk may be drunk or made into cheese

Some or all of the fat in milk can be removed to make skimmed or semi-skimmed varieties

Some yoghurt contains probiotic ("friendly") bacteria

OTHER DAIRY PRODUCTS
Most of the milk produced worldwide is sold as a beverage. The rest is made into dairy products such as cream, buttermilk, butter, cheese, yoghurt, soured cream, condensed milk, powdered milk, ice-cream, and infant formula milk.

Fresh mozzarella is traditionally made with buffalo milk

This goat's cheese is covered in herbs

WHERE DOES MILK COME FROM?
About 90 per cent of the world's milk comes from cows. The rest comes from goats, buffalo, sheep, reindeer, yaks, and other ruminant animals (hoofed animals that chew the cud). In some regions, people prefer goat's milk to cow's milk. It is easier to digest because the protein forms a soft curd and the fat globules do not clump together.

MILKING IT FOR ALL IT'S WORTH
A single cow can produce about 90 glasses of milk a day – but that is just a drop in the bucket in terms of global milk production. Recent estimates put the world's cow milk production at just under five million hectolitres (110 million gallons), and demand for milk, especially in developing countries, is rising. The European Union is the largest milk producer, accounting for almost 25 per cent of world production – the United States produces around 15 per cent.

Italian ice-cream at a gelatteria

Cream inside sealed barrel

Crank turns the churn

ICE-CREAM
One of the most delicious dairy treats, ice-cream, was invented during the 1500s in Italy. There are different types of ice-cream, but in its basic forms ice-cream consists of milk, cream, or custard mixed with sweeteners and flavourings. The mixture is stirred as it is chilled to prevent ice crystals forming.

BUTTER-MAKING
The technique for making butter has been the same for thousands of years. Cream is placed in a sealed container, where it is churned until the microscopic fat globules clump together. The liquid (buttermilk) is drained away, and the butter is washed and put in a mould.

CHEESE-MAKING
The many varieties of cheese are made by culturing milk with bacteria, curdling it with an enzyme called rennet, and separating it from whey, the liquid that forms around the curds. Fresh cheese may be aged to ripen it (above), or sprayed or injected with mould or bacteria for flavour.

COWS AT HOME
Unlike many other food products, milk tends to be produced domestically rather than imported from overseas. Major dairy-producing countries, such as Denmark, France, and Switzerland (above), maintain trade barriers to shut out foreign competition.

Old-fashioned wooden butter churn

Fish and seafood

ALL OVER THE WORLD, people enjoy many types of fish and seafood, as well as sea plants such as sea lettuce and nori (dried seaweed). Fish and seafood are valuable as sources of high-quality protein. Many fish are also rich in the mineral iodine and, if you eat the bones of fish such as sardine, they are a good source of calcium, phosphorus, and fluoride. Eating fatty fish can help us to protect the health of our hearts. Most of the world's fish is caught or harvested through the commercial fishing industry. Its annual world catch is more than a 100 million tonnes. Large quantities are also cultivated through aquaculture ("fish farming"), one of the fastest-growing food industries today.

FISHING IN THE PAST
Since prehistoric times, people have fished the Earth's waters for food. Fishing is depicted in ancient Egyptian tomb paintings and is mentioned in the Bible. Early people used clubs, spears, and nets woven from grass or wool – and even their bare hands – to catch fish. Fish hooks carved from wood and bone were in use about 20,000 years ago.

Prawn

Mussels

Lobster

Paella

SCRUMPTIOUS SEAFOOD
From shark-fin soup to sushi, dishes of fish, shellfish, and seaweed have been important in regional cuisines for centuries. But today, the global demand for seafood is skyrocketing. In addition, fish is no longer a seasonal, local food – fresh seafood is now caught and processed on site, then shipped to fish markets all over the world.

Squid

Lobster stir-fry

SEA CREATURES
Seafood is the catch-all name for ocean animals that are caught and served as food. These include soft-bodied molluscs, such as octopus, squid, mussel, scallop, and cuttlefish, and crustaceans that wear their skeletons on the outside, such as lobster, prawn, and crab. Shellfish are excellent sources of protein and minerals, good sources of B vitamins, and are low in fat. However, some shellfish contain high levels of bacteria, or chemicals as a result of the pollution of the sea by industrial waste.

Crab

Moroccan
trout dish

FRESH-WATER FISH
Fish hauled from lakes, reservoirs,
streams, and rivers are known as
freshwater fish. Some fish, such as carp
and pike, spend their entire lives in fresh
water. Others, such as salmon and trout, are
anadromous, meaning that they live in fresh and
salt water at different stages of life.

Trout

Freshwater
salmon

*Seaweed is
used in salads*

FISH FARMING
Aquaculture (fish farming)
is seen by some as a
solution to the declining
numbers of wild fish. But
its merits are under
debate. Farmed salmon,
for example, may be fed
antibiotics and pink dye.
They may also contain
high levels of pollutants as
a result of being fed
concentrated feed made
from fish living in
polluted water.

MARICULTURE
Cultivating sea plants
in their own habitat is known
as mariculture. Seaweeds and
other marine plants are rich in iodine and
minerals. Nori may be familiar as the green
sheet that is wrapped around sushi.

Salmon sushi

MODERN COMMERCIAL FISHING
Commercial fishing is a huge global industry.
But the industry is facing a critical worldwide
issue: overfishing. Modern fishing ships are
equipped to haul in and process huge
numbers of fish, and there are now simply
too many of these ships catching too
many fish. Fish populations are in
steep decline, as nations fight over
the right to fish what is left.

Food dangers

MANY FOODS WE EAT TODAY come with a side order of risk. The dangers arising from modern food production make for a fairly unsavoury list. They include residues from pesticides, or drugs and hormones given to livestock, food-borne micro-organisms and parasites, and mercury or other metals, any of which might end up in the food on our plate. We are told that we must accept certain levels of chemical contamination, since industrialized farming depends on chemicals to produce food. But what levels are safe? And when these chemicals build up in our body tissues, what is the long-term effect on health? Recent scares such as avian 'flu and "mad cow disease" have also raised consumer awareness about food dangers.

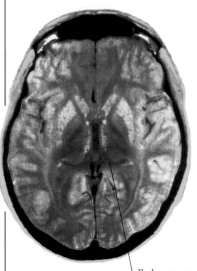

Red areas are diseased

CREUTZFELDT-JAKOB DISEASE (CJD)
This is a brain scan of a young man suffering from CJD, who later died. It is thought that eating beef from cows with bovine spongiform encephalopathy (BSE, or "mad cow disease") can cause CJD. BSE is caused by an infectious agent called a prion that builds up in the brain and spinal cord of infected cows. It came about from the practice of feeding cows with infected sheep carcasses.

GROWTH HORMONES
Animals, such as this cow, are injected with growth hormones to increase meat or milk yield. There are worries that hormones are not only dangerous to the animals, but also to the humans who eat the meat.

INDUSTRIAL WASTE
There are concerns about the safety of eating seafood that has been contaminated with industrial waste. These Japanese people are protesting about a company accused of dumping mercury compounds into Minamata Bay, Japan, in the 1950s and '60s. Seafood was polluted with mercury, leading to an epidemic of poisoning that sickened or killed thousands.

Geese and chickens packed into baskets on their way to market

UNDER WRAPS
Packaging materials such as clingfilm and polystyrene trays contribute to food safety by protecting and preserving fresh food. But there are concerns that any packaging in contact with food may also contaminate it with small amounts of residual chemicals. Food packaging materials must comply with a complex set of national laws aimed at ensuring that food safety is not compromised.

FOOD COLOURINGS
Artificial colourings are added to many foods – especially sweets and other products marketed to children – to make them look appealing. There is concern about the effect of consuming high levels of colourings and other additives on health. Some food colourings are known to cause behavioural problems in children.

TOO CLOSE FOR COMFORT
When lots of animals are kept in close proximity, the risk of bacteria or viruses spreading between them increases. Humans who are in close contact with animals can also become infected. In 2003, avian 'flu (spread from human contact with live, infected birds) hit the Far East. This is a particularly lethal strain of 'flu.

BACTERIA IN FOOD

Harmful bacteria can cause a range of sicknesses from food poisoning to some types of cancer. The worst offenders are *Salmonella*, *Campylobacter*, *E. coli*, and *Clostridium botulinum*. In 2002, one survey found *Campylobacter* bacteria in about 50 per cent of raw chicken on sale in the UK.

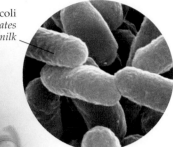

E. coli
*contaminates
beef and milk*

E. coli

*Yellow rods
are bacteria*

Salmonella enteritidis

*Whip-like
tails help
bacteria move*

Campylobacter
jejuni

MICRO-ORGANISMS IN FOOD

Wherever food is produced, processed, or stored, there are micro-organisms – viruses, yeast, moulds, bacteria and parasites. While these may not cause illness in small numbers, they can pose a threat to health if they multiply. This is why food suppliers should store foods such as meat in chilled rooms and check the temperature regularly.

MOULD TOXINS

Moulds are fungi that live on plants and animals. You might see a few white flecks of mould on old bread, but this fungi also has very long roots that grow deep into the food. Some types of mould can make us ill. Aflatoxin, for example, is a toxic mould that grows on peanuts (right) and field corn. It is known to cause cancer in animals.

SPRAYING CROPS WITH PESTICIDE

The full health risks associated with pesticides are uncertain. While reports show that in most cases pesticide levels in foods are well within acceptable safety limits, many experts say that it is impossible to predict the dangers of the "cocktail effect" (the impact of a mixture of different pesticides) on our health in the long-term. Some recent research suggests that exposure to pesticides may be linked with leukaemia and brain cancer, and increased rates of cancer among farmers.

The GM debate

THE FATHER OF GENETICS
Gregor Mendel (1822–1884) was an Austrian monk who discovered the basic laws of heredity. From 1858 to 1866, he bred garden peas in his monastery garden. Mendel noted that certain traits (such as pod shape or flower colour) were passed down from "parent" plants to their offspring. Although he is now referred to as the father of genetics, Mendel's work did not have an impact until long after his death.

WE LIVE IN A HIGH-TECH WORLD and soon we may all be eating high-tech food. Genetically modified (GM) foods are the first agricultural products of a branch of science known as biotechnology. GM foods are developed by altering the genetic material in cells to add a desired trait to a food. This can be done by adding a gene from the same species – for example, adding a tomato gene from a frost-resistant plant into another tomato plant. Or a gene can cross species – for example, adding a gene from a fish that survives in very cold water to a tomato plant to make it frost-resistant. GM foods have caused enormous controversy. In the US, most people have accepted GM foods, but the EU has only recently allowed them.

Non-GM tomatoes

GM tomatoes

Over-ripe fruit is difficult to ship – and to sell

THE RISE IN GM CROPS
A 2004 global study showed that there are 67.7 million hectares (167.2 million acres) planted with GM crops. Seven million farmers in 18 different countries grow GM crops. An estimated 99 per cent of these crops are grown in just six countries: the US, Argentina, Canada, China, Brazil, and South Africa. The most common GM crops are soya beans, maize, and cotton and rape seeds (used to make oil).

Plantlets cultured from a single cell

Flavr Savr tomato plantlets

LONG-LIFE TOMATOES
In early 1994, the US Food and Drug Administration (FDA) determined that the "Flavr Savr", a genetically modified tomato, was as safe as tomatoes bred by conventional means. Flavr Savr became the first fresh genetically modified crop sold in the world. It was modified to stay fresh and intact for longer than non-GM tomatoes during harvesting and transportation.

This corn is modified to tolerate herbicides

THE KEY TO GM FOODS

A basic unit of genetic material is a gene, and genes are made of a substance called DNA (deoxyribonucleic acid). DNA contains the chemical instructions for building and maintaining life. Genetic engineers can modify an existing part of DNA, or introduce a new gene into an organism to alter its characteristics.

Computer model of DNA

THE PERILS OF POLLEN

One concern over GM crops is the danger of cross-pollination with non-GM plants. Insects, birds, and the wind can carry seeds and pollen from GM plants into neighbouring fields and beyond. If cross-pollination occurs, consumers and farmers no longer have a choice about whether or not to support GM foods.

Micrograph of cotton pollen

PUBLIC REACTION

In many parts of the world, GM foods remain controversial, for the reasons outlined below. These environmental activists are destroying a GM test crop (oil-seed rape) in Oxfordshire, UK.

BANANA CURE

At present, crops are genetically modified for two reasons: to resist pests or to tolerate herbicides. But in the future, fruit and vegetables could be used as a medium in which to grow other products, such as drugs. South African scientists have used GM techniques to modify bananas to incorporate a vaccine for the deadly disease cholera.

THE ARGUMENT FOR GM FOODS

- GM foods could mean a reduction in the use of pesticides, as resistance to pests is built in genetically.

- GM foods could be farmed in places where conventional crops would fail.

- Fruit and vegetables could be turned into delivery methods for vaccines.

- Foods such as GM corn (below), may help feed a growing population.

- GM crops could boost prosperity in the developing world.

- Forty per cent of the world's food crop is lost every year to insects, disease, and spoilage. Resistant GM crops could limit this.

- GM might improve our food, enhancing its taste, extending its shelf-life, and making it more nutritious.

- Intensive farming has already harmed the countryside in many places and GM may offer a better way to manage the land.

GM Corn on the cob

THE ARGUMENT AGAINST GM FOODS

- There has been no long-term safety testing. We do not know how these foods will affect our health or how they will affect the environment.

- Gene pollution cannot be cleaned up. Once it's out there, it's out there.

Parsnip seeds

- GM foods may contain previously unknown allergens.

- Seeds from a GM crop (above right) will be identical, so if a fungus or pest develops that can attack the seeds, the entire crop will fail.

- Big bio-tech companies are focusing on the profitable GM crops (maize, cotton, and soya), rather than GM rice and cassava that would help tackle the issue of starvation in Africa.

- Traditional farmers save seeds from a harvest to plant the next year. But bio-tech companies force farmers growing GM crops to buy new supplies every year, trapping them in a never-ending cycle of dependency.

Why organic?

OUTSTANDING IN HIS FIELD
A pioneering voice in the organic farming movement, American author and publisher J. I. Rodale (1898–1971) and his wife Anna developed and demonstrated farming methods that helped increase soil fertility. His 1942 book, *Organic Farming and Gardening*, popularized the idea of organic farming in the United States.

ORGANIC FOOD describes food that is produced using organic farming methods. This means that no long-lasting chemical pesticides or fertilizers are sprayed on growing crops, and livestock is raised without hormones and antibiotics. Land must also be farmed organically for two years before crops may be labelled organic. Legally, organic foods must come from growers, processors, and importers who have been formally approved by a government body. Organic foods account for about 1–2 per cent of worldwide food sales. In recent years, concerns about food safety, environmental pollution, and GM crops have increased consumer interest in organic foods. Today, organic food products represent the fastest-growing segment of food sales. Yet debate continues as to whether organic food really is better for our health.

COMPANION PLANTING
Many plants have substances in their roots, flowers, or leaves that attract or repel certain insects. Planting two crops together helps to control pests naturally without the need for pesticides. Here, the bright colours of the flowers attract pests that might otherwise eat the bean plants.

MAKING COMPOST
Compost is an excellent natural fertilizer that organic farmers use to improve soil quality naturally. It consists of plant matter that has been allowed to decompose with the help of insects, earthworms, bacteria, and fungi. As well as making soil fertile and nutritious, compost is also a useful way to recycle plant waste such as grass clippings and autumn leaves.

Rhubarb leaves and stalks are added to compost

TRADITIONAL METHODS
Rather than being kept in a cage, these chickens are reared on an organic diet and allowed to roam freely in the fresh air and sunshine. This is how chickens would have been kept on a traditional farm of the 1900s. Few organic farming and animal husbandry ideas are new. They tend to be similar to the ways in which food was produced before mass agricultural modernization.

GIVING CONSUMERS A CHOICE

Organic food is now found in many markets and supermarkets, some of which are completely dedicated to organic foods, such as this store in Tours, France. Many people believe that organic food has more flavour than the non-organic equivalent.

Fresh, seasonal produce is delivered to the door

DELIVERING NATURE'S BOUNTY

Innovations such as Community Supported Agriculture (CSA) programmes are helping to bring organic food to everyone. In some programmes, people make a cash investment in a farmer's crops at the beginning of the growing season. When the crops are harvested, each investor receives a weekly basket of produce.

ORGANIC LABELLING LAWS

In Europe, producers must comply with strict laws before labelling food as organic. However, even organic foods may contain some non-organic ingredients – not all foods are available in organic form yet. If a food is made from 95 per cent organic ingredients, it can be labelled organic. If 70–95 per cent of ingredients are organic, the word "organic" may appear only in the ingredients list.

ORGANIC BABY FOOD

Some parents choose to feed babies and children with organic food because they prefer not to expose them to chemicals in food, such as pesticides. Regulations about the amount of pesticide residues that are allowed in non-organic foods are based on acceptable levels for adult consumption only.

Demand for prepared organic baby food is on the rise

ORGANIC OR NOT?

Evidence is emerging that organic foods may contain higher levels of some vitamins and phytochemicals (beneficial substances found in plant foods such as garlic). Organic farming methods have been shown to have benefits for the environment. For example, soil pollution from pesticides is reduced and biodiversity (the number and range of plant and animal species) is supported.

Organic garlic

Non-organic garlic

Feeding the world

THE WORLD POPULATION is expected to increase from six billion people today to nine billion by 2050. This raises the question of how to provide food for everyone in the world without destroying the environment in the process. There is no clear answer. Intensive farmers say their methods will produce the most crops in the available land. On the other side of the debate are organic farmers who say that intensive farming will destroy the land and only delay mass starvation – organic methods will keep the land fertile. Many people advocate education, giving farmers information and access to modern technology. Even more crucial, a fair way of sharing the world's food must be found.

FAMINE THROUGHOUT HISTORY
Famine occurs when a country or area does not have enough food or resources to feed its people. It is not a new problem. Famine was so common in the ancient world that one of the Four Horsemen of the Apocalypse (above) in the Bible was named Famine.

A CRITICAL TIME OF LIFE
Food shortages are devastating for all, but some groups of people are particularly at risk: pregnant women, new mothers and their children, and elderly people. Children whose bodies have been weakened by hunger, like this child in Sudan, are highly vulnerable to disease.

FOOD SHORTAGES
These Sudanese people at a refugee camp are queuing up for food distributed by the World Food Programme. Although there is currently enough food to feed everyone on the planet, more than 800 million people (13 per cent of the world's population) go to bed hungry every night, and 24,000 people die every day from hunger and related causes. These numbers are rising. Hunger continues to be one of the main challenges we face today and in the future.

HUNGER IN EMERGENCIES
Poverty, war, and civil unrest can give rise to food shortages, but they can also arise as a result of natural disasters. Floods, drought, crop failure, hurricanes, and earthquakes (as seen in this 1985 picture of a devastated Mexico City) create sudden food shortages. Many years of development – from roads and bridges to schools and hospitals – can be wiped out in a matter of minutes.

WHEAT

NOT TO BE SOLD OR EXCHANGED

USE NO HOOKS

FOOD AID

Countries that produce an excess of food may offer food aid to other nations, through government-sponsored or private organizations. Food aid may be in the form of offering grants or loans so that developing nations can buy food, or providing food directly, as in this French delivery to Somalia.

INTENSIVE FARMING

One possible solution to the global food crisis is to produce more food through the intensive farming of crops and livestock (such as battery hens, above). Experts are divided about the best way to balance the demands of a growing market with environmental concerns.

Mouse makes its home in the wheat

Harvest mouse

DAMAGE TO WILDLIFE

Supporters of intensive farming argue that using modern machines and genetically modified crops is the best way to get the most from the land. But the environmental effects of a massive increase in farming are uncertain. Many animals, such as the harvest mouse, already face extinction due to combine harvesting.

EDUCATION

One way to help farmers in developing nations is through sharing knowledge. Educating farmers around the world and giving them access to technology may help put more food in hungry mouths in the long term. These farmers and their teacher in Somalia are working on ways to re-start agriculture in their village.

Did you know?

AMAZING FACTS

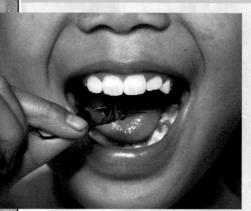

Child about to snack on an insect, Thailand

Insects are a popular snack in many countries. Bug-eaters enjoy termites, fried or dried grasshoppers, crickets, locusts, and smoked caterpillars. Most insects are high in protein and low in fat.

Earthworms are high in protein and contain heart-healthy oils. They must be soaked before eating to remove dirt.

The Australian honey ant stores honey in the swollen globe of its rear end. People bite the bottoms to get to the sweet treat. Honey bees are also eaten.

Rotten fish have been, and still are, eaten in many cultures. The ancient Romans used garum (salty rotten fish guts) as seasoning. In ancient China, cooks let fish go off in milk to make *cha* – eaten in thin slices. Norwegian cooks bury trout in salt and sugar for several months to make Rakorret. The Vietnamese bury fish in salt – the fish digest themselves with their own stomach fluids to make the seasoning sauce, *nuoc mam*.

The world's supply of nests for a delicacy known as bird's nest soup is found in a tiny region of S.E. Asia. The swiftlet nests (below) are made of hardened bird saliva. They can be reached only by climbing high up on vines and bamboo (right).

Swiftlet nests

Harvesting the nests

American "cowboy coffee" was made by putting coffee grounds in a clean sock placed in water and boiled over a fire.

Throughout history, salt has been one of the world's most valuable commodities. It was even used as currency in the Roman empire. Salt was a luxury that was often taxed – the Great Wall of China was paid for in part with taxes from the state monopoly on salt. In British colonial India, a salt tax eventually led Gandhi and thousands of others to march to the sea to get untaxed salt.

Some ancient Chinese ate live baby rats, and Romans raised dormice for snacks. Incas ate guinea pigs and squirrels. Opossums and muskrats are traditional foods in parts of America and Canada.

During the Age of Exploration (late 1400s to early 1800s), sailors who had no fresh meat ate rats.

Coffee beans

Diners at a wealthy person's banquet in the Middle Ages might encounter a peacock and swan looking very much alive. The birds were killed, carefully skinned to keep the feathers intact, cooked, and stuffed back into their skins. Their beaks and feet may even have been covered with gold. Live birds were sometimes put into a baked piecrust to fly out when the crust was cut, just as in the nursery rhyme *Sing a Song of Sixpence*.

Feeling chirpy? Spring robins on toast appeared in US breakfasts as recently as the American Civil War (1861–65).

Cannibalism has been practised at various times throughout history. In an Aztec sacrifice, the heart of the victim was offered to the gods. The rest of the body was divided up, stewed with maize and salt, and eaten. This was not an ordinary meal, but connected to a religious ceremony and therefore strictly controlled.

The colonists who settled America faced severe food shortages. During the period known as the Starving Time (1609–1610), Captain John Smith reported that one of the colonists resorted to eating his wife. The man was executed when his crime was discovered – but robbing graves for food was also common.

People in other desperate situations – John Franklin's polar expedition and, more recently, the Uruguayan rugby team members who survived a plane crash – have resorted to cannibalism, but, in general, historians believe people have been accused of the act more often than it has been committed.

Before people drank coffee, they chewed the leaves and red berries of the coffee tree. In the 9th century, coffee beans were ground into a paste with animal fat. Muslim pilgrims, grateful that coffee kept them awake during their prayers, spread coffee across the globe.

Coffee houses appeared all over Europe in the 1600s. Enthusiasm for the drink was widespread, although it was scorned by the governing classes. The French tried to ban it because they thought it would replace wine as the national beverage – the Germans feared for their beer.

The origin of tea as a medicinal herb useful for staying awake is unclear. The use of tea as a beverage drunk for pleasure on social occasions dates from the Chinese Tang Dynasty (618–907CE) or earlier. The first Europeans to encounter tea were Portuguese explorers visiting Japan in 1560. Soon, imported tea was introduced to Europe, where it quickly became popular among the wealthy in France and the Netherlands, and later Britain. Tea was far more popular than coffee in the American colonies, and coffee more popular than tea back in England. When the British put a tax on tea, the colonists revolted by dumping crates of British tea into the Boston harbour.

Monks were responsible for tending the vineyards in France. One monk experimented with methods of producing the famous French sparkling wine, champagne. His name? Dom Perignon.

In ancient Egypt, adults and children alike drank beer at mealtimes. This fermentation of dates and barley bread was a thick soupy liquid – very nutritious, and not very alcoholic. It was also far safer to drink than water from the river Nile, which could give you intestinal worms!

Most people have encountered the occasional wormy apple, but in truth nearly every food we eat contains insects, albeit in tiny amounts. Food standards regulations acknowledge the presence of insect fragments or larvae and set small but acceptable limits. We may be eating a kilo of bugs a year without knowing it!

QUESTIONS AND ANSWERS

Q What are the most expensive foods and drinks in the world?

A Beluga caviar (the eggs of the beluga sturgeon fish – usually Russian) is often included in lists of the world's most expensive foods. Saffron is the world's costliest spice. To harvest it, workers remove three tiny tips from a type of crocus blossom. It takes 225,000 tips to make 0.45kg (1lb) of saffron. Truffles are the most expensive fungi. Some animals (pigs and dogs) can sniff them out while they are still buried underground. Kopi Luwak coffee costs about 50 times more than other coffees – the beans are special because they are first digested by a cat-like animal called a palm civet, and are then collected from its droppings!

Saffron on stamen

Crocus flower

Q What are the staple foods eaten around the world?

A There are approximately 50,000 edible plants on Earth, but just three of these crops – rice, maize, and wheat – provide 60 per cent of the world's food energy. Other staple foods include millet, sorghum, and roots and tubers (such as potatoes, cassava, yams, and taro), complemented by animal proteins such as meat, fish, cheese, and eggs.

Q Who are the main food providers across the globe?

A For every farmer in the developed world, there are 19 farmers in the developing world. Women usually play an important role in providing food. In the developing world, for example, women and children are often entirely responsible for growing food for their households.

Q What wild foods do people gather and eat?

A Fish is by far the world's largest wild food harvest. It is a major source of protein for an incredible 1,000 million people. Other sources of protein that people gather from the wild are insects, birds, frogs, rodents, and larger mammals. People also collect and eat forest foods such as leaves, fruit, seeds, and nuts. In some rural areas (for example, in Swaziland), people eat more wild plant foods than cultivated ones.

Q How much food does the average person eat?

A Every day about 11.5 litres (20 pints) of digested food, liquids, and digestive juices flow through the digestive system, but only about 100ml (one sixth of a pint) of this is lost in faeces. We each eat about 500kg (half a ton) of food per year, although this varies according to the part of the world in which we live. In poor countries where people are undernourished, food intake may be substantially less.

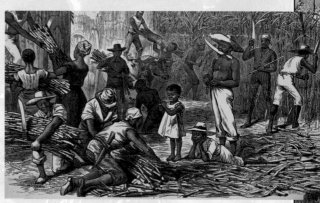

Slaves working on a sugar plantation

Record Breakers

- **LARGEST BOX OF CHOCOLATES**
  A box made in 2002 by the Frango Mint Co in Chicago, US, held 90,090 chocolates.

- **LARGEST COOKIE**
  A chocolate chip cookie created in Christchurch, New Zealand, in 1996 measured 24.9m (81ft) in diameter.

- **LARGEST BAGEL**
  In 1998, Lender's Bagels in Illinois, USA made a bagel weighing 323kg (714lb).

- **HOTTEST PEPPER**
  The Red Savina Habanero is 50 times hotter than the jalapeno.

- **BIGGEST FOOD FIGHT**
  The tomato fight at La Tomatina festival in Spain.

La Tomatina tomato fight

Some 12 tonnes of tomatoes are used

Q When did people start eating sugar?

A As early as 800BCE, people in India learned how to remove the juice from the sugarcane stalk and dry it, leaving only the sweet crystals of sugar behind. The Arabs introduced sugar to Europe, where it was prized as a medicine. Apothecaries shaved flakes off cones of sugar and sold them – sugar flakes were thought to be the ideal remedy for toothache. By the middle of the 1700s, sugar was a food staple even for the poor. Slaves worked day and night to grow, harvest, and process sugar on vast plantations in the Caribbean.

Timeline

Here is a timeline of some important events in the world's food history. You will see how developments in cuisine have shaped food trends in society, which foods have "migrated" far from their native continents, and how important innovations and inventions have changed the way we eat – from the taming of fire to the introduction of the microwave oven.

Ancient hunters spear and club a bear

400,000BCE
Early humans have a diet of wild plants, roots, nuts, acorns, legumes, and wild grains. Hunters can track down and kill some animals.

75,000BCE
Neanderthal man is a skilled hunter, able to bring down mammoths and sabre-toothed tigers.

35,000BCE
Humans can now control fire. Their superior intelligence allows them to hunt for more food, with better tools.

25,000BCE
Food is cooked in small pits dug in the ground, lined with hot embers or pebbles.

12,000BCE
Tribespeople in the lower Nile use knives to harvest wild grass and grind flour from it. Potters in Japan make clay storage and cooking pots.

10,000BCE
Goats are domesticated in the Near East.

8000BCE The seeds of wild grains are cultivated in the Near East. Nomadic people begin to settle in communities.

A domestic goat

5000BCE
Rice cultivation begins in China's Yangtze River delta.

2800BCE
Sumerian farmers invent the sickle – a tool with a semicircular blade. This will remain the prominent tool for harvesting grain for thousands of years.

2500BCE
Workers toiling on the Great Pyramid of Khufu in Egypt are sustained by chickpeas, onions, fish, and garlic.

1500BCE
Almost all the major food plants we know today are cultivated somewhere in the world at this time.

350BCE
The first cookbook is written by Greek author Archestratus.

312BCE
Rome gets fresh drinking water from an aqueduct connecting the city to hillside springs.

400
Anthimus, a Greek physician, issues dietary advice to Christians in *The Dietetics*. He argues that foods should be chosen according to how digestible they are. He warns against eating bacon rind, pigeon, and mushrooms, amongst other things.

1250
European crusaders returning from the Middle East bring cardamom, cinnamon, cloves, coriander, cumin, ginger, mace, saffron, and nutmeg to Europe.

1400
Italian shops make pasta commercially. Up until now it has been a luxury food.

1492
Italian explorer Christopher Columbus discovers New World foods such as sweet potatoes, peppers, plantain, and maize.

1510
Sunflowers from America are brought to Europe. They soon become a major oilseed crop.

1519
An officer with Cortés (the Spanish conqueror) reports that the Aztec emperor Montezuma drinks 50 flagons of chocolate a day.

1525
Chillies from the Americas are introduced to India.

1530
A Spanish explorer in the Andes, South America, encounters the potato, which will become Europe's staple crop.

1561
Marmalade is created by a physician to Mary Queen of Scots to settle her stomach on a sea crossing from France to Scotland.

1582
Coffee is mentioned for the first time in print, by a European merchant who travelled to Arabia.

1610
The first mention of bagels, in Poland.

1621
Pilgrims and Native Americans celebrate the first Thanksgiving in America.

1634
To ensure top quality mustard, France imposes strict rules on mustard makers.

1652
London's first coffee house opens – within 10 years, there will be thousands.

1661
London's Covent Garden market becomes a fruit, vegetable, and flower market.

1677
The French establish vast cacao plantations in Brazil.

1681
The pressure cooker is invented in France.

1689
An Italian physician encourages people to drink walnut juice. He says that it promotes health and longevity.

1702
A sushi shop opens in Japan.

1723
Coffee plants are first grown in Martinique, in the Caribbean.

1729
The satire *A Modest Proposal* by Irish writer Jonathan Swift advocates eating children to ease the Irish population crisis.

1764
France's first public restaurant opens.

1762
The English Earl of Sandwich invents the sandwich.

Sandwiches are lunchtime staples

1769
A Spanish Franciscan missionary, Junipero Serra, plants the first wine grapes, oranges, figs, and olives in California.

1774
English explorer James Cook nearly dies of poisoning after eating a blowfish.

1785
Scottish poet Robert Burns writes a poem celebrating the haggis.

1790
Pineapples are introduced to Hawaii by a Spanish adventurer.

1805
US inventor Oliver Evans designs the first refrigeration machine.

1809
Frenchman Nicolas Appert invents vacuum packing – food is boiled in jars, then sealed with corks and tar.

1812
First known recipe for tomato ketchup.

1845
Ireland's potato crop fails and causes widespread famine.

1824
The first commercial pasta factory is built in Italy.

1826
The first commercially practicable gas stove is designed in England.

1838
The Dutch chemist Gerard Mulder coins the word "protein".

1850
The American Vegetarian Society is founded.

1853
Potato crisps are invented at Saratoga Springs, New York. A restaurant customer complains that the chips are too thick and gets wafer-thin fried potatoes instead.

1859
Voluntary starvation – anorexia nervosa – is first recognized as a disease. It tends to affect young women between the ages of 16 and 23.

1868
Tabasco brand hot sauce is formulated in Louisiana, US.

1869
British grocer Sainsbury's begins business.

1876
Heinz tomato ketchup is introduced.

1883
The luxury train, the Orient Express, first departs Paris, France for Constantinople, Turkey, with restaurant cars serving the finest cuisine.

1885
Salmonella bacteria is first described.

1893
The breakfast cereal Shredded Wheat is introduced.

1895
The word "calorie" is applied to food by US chemist Wilbur Atwater.

1897
Campbell's condensed soup is invented in the US. You just add water and heat.

1900
Milk starts being sold in bottles in England.

1901
Several oat milling pioneers in the Midwest of America unite to form Quaker Oats Incorporated.

1903
Peanut butter is introduced as a health food.

1907
Canada Dry Ginger Ale is registered as a trademark.

Quaker oats

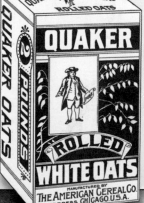

1916
Coca-Cola adopts its distinctive bottle shape, said to resemble the coca leaf or kola nut.

1929
Unilever (the first multinational food company) is established.

1939
The Ministry of Food is established in Britain.

1941
The first recommended dietary allowances (RDAs) are introduced in the US telling people how much of each nutrient they need for good health.

1953
First Swanson TV dinner.

1955
American restaurant pioneer Ray Kroc opens his first McDonald's burger stand. Colonel Sanders promotes Kentucky Fried Chicken.

1982
Egg substitutes hit the market as concerns grew about egg yolks and cholesterol.

Coca-Cola

MID-1980s
Microwavable products rise in popularity as microwave oven ownership soars.

1986
"Mad cow" disease scare begins in Britain. The Slow Food movement is founded in Italy to promote the enjoyment of wholesome foods.

1997
A sheep named Dolly is cloned from an udder cell of an adult sheep.

1999
The first UK-wide Internet grocers promises home delivery of food and other goods ordered online.

2000
The Betasweet carrot, bred to be a powerful antioxidant, is sold in Texas, US.

2001
Foot and mouth disease devastates livestock farming in the UK.

2004
The European Union lifts its ban on genetically modified (GM) crops. GM foods must be labelled.

Find out more

FOOD IS ESSENTIAL TO THE LIFE of every human being on the planet. Here is how to find out more about the ways in which people get their daily bread, tortilla, rice, or chapati. Science museums contain exhibits related to agriculture as well as to food and nutrition. Plan a visit to a working farm, or visit a living history farm dedicated to a specific agricultural era. Get an insider view of food production by taking a factory tour. An exploration of a local ethnic shop will remind you that what is exotic to some people is everyday fare for others.

Production line at a biscuit factory

TAKE A FACTORY TOUR
The closest you can get to a real food production line without applying for a job is taking a factory tour. Check the Internet to find a tour in your area. Although you may not be able to see the entire factory, you will definitely get a feel for the sheer scale of modern food production – and you may get a food sample, as well!

VISIT A WORKING FARM
There are hundreds of working farms across the United Kingdom. The Internet or local tourism boards will direct you to a farm. You can visit for a day, or plan a holiday on a working farm to experience first hand what living off the land is like. Springtime visits to see the newborn animals are especially popular.

Sprouting beans and seeds is easy and fast

Durian fruit from S.E. Asia

"Grow" food without a garden – bean sprouts

GROW YOUR OWN FOOD
How does your garden grow? There is only one way to find out. If you want to try your hand at growing food, and you are lucky enough to have a garden, give it a go. Even a window box can provide herbs to give flavour to food. Pick up a gardening guide at your local library or bookshop for step-by-step instructions, or get recommendations at your local garden centre.

ETHNIC GROCERY STORES
If you live in or visit a multi-ethnic neighbourhood, you can get a taste of the cuisine of a faraway culture in a nearby shop. Browse the aisles to check out unusual spices, fruit, vegetables, or tinned goods. A visit to a market that features stalls catering to a wide variety of people can also introduce you to new foods. Try something you have never eaten before!

Places to Visit

SCIENCE MUSEUM, LONDON
Visit the Food for Thought gallery, which examines how science and technology affect the food we eat.

GODSTONE FARM, SURREY
Encounter a wide range of farm animals, including cows, pigs, sheep, goats, and chickens, at close range.

CADBURY WORLD, BIRMINGHAM
Discover the history of chocolate, from the Aztecs to now.

BOROUGH MARKET, LONDON
See a selection of fine local food products from every region of the country. Opens every Saturday morning.

MUSEUM OF SCOTTISH COUNTRY LIFE, EAST KILBRIDE
Step into a complete, working 1950s farmhouse at this museum.

NATIONAL MUSEUM OF WALES, CARDIFF
View a collection of agricultural implements that date from the late 18th century to modern times.

BEAMISH, THE NORTH OF ENGLAND OPEN AIR MUSEUM, CO. DURHAM
Discover how a large farm was run in 1913.

AGROPOLIS MUSEUM, MONTPELLIER, FRANCE
This science centre takes a historical approach to foods from all over the world.

ALIMENTARIUM FOOD MUSEUM, VEVY, SWITZERLAND
Here you can see the complete story of food, from farm to table. Visit the large open-plan kitchen for demonstrations.

Egyptian farm labourer, British Museum

Pick used to break up rocky soil

Museum model of digestive organs

VISITING MUSEUMS
Many museums feature large and comprehensive exhibits dedicated to agricultural history. From an ancient scythe to the latest in harvesting, you will be able to trace the evolution of agricultural technology and find out what effects these machines had on the food supply.

SOMETHING TO DIGEST
Human body exhibits at many science museums focus on how we digest, absorb, and use food as fuel for life. Models, displays, and interactive exhibits help explain the workings of the human digestive system and how it changes food into energy.

Glossary

ADDITIVE A substance added to food and drink for a specific purpose, for example, as a preservative. Additives are not natural parts of food.

AGRICULTURE The practice or business of cultivating the land.

ALLERGY An abnormal reaction of the body to a substance that is normally harmless to other people in a similar amount.

AMINO ACIDS The basic building blocks of proteins. Amino acids are essential to human metabolism.

ANIMAL HUSBANDRY The business of a farmer in raising and caring for livestock.

ANTIOXIDANTS Substances found in fruit, vegetables, and other plant foods that prevent oxidation.

AQUACULTURE The practice of using the sea, lakes, or rivers for fish or shellfish cultivation.

BACTERIA A class of microscopic organisms that may cause disease.

BASAL METABOLIC RATE The amount of energy the body needs to function while at rest.

BETA-CAROTENE A nutrient found in yellow and orange fruit and vegetables. The body converts it into vitamin A.

BILE A thick, bitter fluid that aids digestion and is secreted by the liver.

BIOFLAVONOID A group of phytochemicals in plant foods. They have health benefits, such as protecting against cancer.

Blueberries contain antioxidants

BRAN The tough, indigestible outer husks of wheat, rice, oats, and other grains. Bran provides a rich source of fibre in the diet.

CALCIUM A mineral that we need for healthy teeth and bones.

CALORIE A unit that is used to express the amount of energy contained within a food.

CANNING A method of food preservation in which foods are sealed in airtight tins.

CARBOHYDRATE The sugars and starches that form the main source of energy in the diet.

CARCINOGEN A substance that causes cancer.

CARNIVORE A flesh-eating animal.

CASEIN A protein in milk that solidifies during cheese-making.

CHOLESTEROL A waxy, fat-like compound that is present in food and which is also manufactured by the liver. Excess cholesterol may lead to narrowing of the arteries that supply blood to the heart.

COMPLETE PROTEIN A protein that contains all of the essential amino acids. Meat, fish, and eggs provide complete protein.

COMPLEX CARBOHYDRATE A chain of glucose molecules, also known as starches. Starches are the form in which plants store their energy.

Complex carbohydrates

Calcium crystals

CRUSTACEA A class of animals with hard shells, including crabs, lobsters, and prawns.

CUISINE The style of cooking common to a particular region or country.

CURING A method of food preservation in which food is dried, salted, or smoked.

DAIRY The collective name for milk and milk products, for example, cheese, butter, and yoghurt.

DIETARY REFERENCE VALUE (DRV) The amount of energy or nutrient that a group of people of a specific age (for example, babies) need for good health.

DIGESTION The process by which food is broken down in the body and converted to forms that can be absorbed into the bloodstream and delivered to cells.

DIGESTIVE TRACT The passage from the mouth to the anus in which food is digested and absorbed.

DRYING A method of food preservation in which water and other liquids are removed.

ENERGY The power required for the body to function and move. Food energy is measured in calories.

ENZYME A protein substance that speeds up chemical reactions in the body.

ESSENTIAL FATTY ACIDS A class of fatty acids that we need to get from food because we cannot manufacture them by ourselves. Essential fatty acids fall into two groups: omega-3 and omega-6.

Essential fatty acid: linolenic acid

FAMINE An extreme scarcity of food.

FAT A nutrient that supplies a concentrated source of energy to the body.

FIBRE Compounds in plant foods that are not easily digested by the body.

FOOD A substance that contains essential nutrients.

FOOD GUIDE PYRAMID An illustrated guide to a balanced diet proposed by the US Food and Drug Administration in 1992.

FOOD WEB A series of organisms connected by the fact that each forms food for the next organism in the web.

FREE RADICAL Disease-causing substances that are produced during oxidation.

GALLBLADDER The bile-storing sac attached to the liver.

GLUCOSE The basic unit of carbohydrates. Glucose is present in fruit and plant juices, and in the blood of animals.

GLYCAEMIC INDEX A means of classifying carbohydrate foods according to how quickly they release glucose into the blood.

GLYCOGEN The form in which glucose is stored in the liver and muscles.

HALAL Meat killed according to Islamic law.

HERBIVORE A plant-eating animal.

IMMUNE SYSTEM The body's defence mechanism that protects us from disease-causing micro-organisms.

INCOMPLETE PROTEIN A protein source that lacks some essential amino acids.

INSULIN A hormone that regulates the level of glucose in the blood.

IRON A mineral that helps transport oxygen in red blood cells.

IRRADIATION Exposing food to radiation to kill micro-organisms.

KILOCALORIE 1,000 calories, used to measure the energy value of food.

LACTOVEGETARIAN A diet in which plant foods are eaten along with milk and milk products.

LARGE INTESTINE The wider tube that food enters after leaving the small intestine during digestion.

LEGUME A food with a seed pod. For example, peas and beans.

LIPIDS A group of compounds including fats, oils, and waxes.

LIVER A large organ that stores glucose (as glycogen), secretes bile, and filters blood.

MAIZE A corn-like staple cereal.

MINERAL An element that the body needs for growth and repair and bodily processes.

MOLLUSC A soft-bodied creature that usually has a shell. For example, mussels.

MONOUNSATURATED FAT A type of fat that is usually liquid at room temperature and solid or semi-solid when refrigerated. For example, oils made from olives or nuts.

MONOSODIUM GLUTAMATE (MSG) A white crystalline salt used in food as a flavour enhancer.

NUTRIENT A substance found in food that is needed for life and growth.

NUTRITIONIST A person who studies foods and its nutritional content.

OESOPHAGUS The pipe that transports food from the mouth to the stomach.

ORGANIC Food produced without the use of artificial fertilizers or pesticides, or other chemicals.

OVOLACTOVEGETARIAN A diet in which plant foods are eaten along with eggs, milk, and milk products.

OXIDATION The chemical process by which body cells burn food in the presence of oxygen.

PANCREAS A large gland that secretes digestive juices.

PHOTOSYNTHESIS The method by which green plants make food with sunlight, carbon dioxide, and water.

PHYTOCHEMICALS A range of health-protecting substances found in plant foods.

PICKLING A method of food preservation using salt or vinegar.

POLYUNSATURATED FAT A type of fat that is usually liquid at room temperature. For example, vegetable oils such as corn oil.

Vegan foods

PROTEIN A chain of amino acids. Proteins are essential for growth and repair.

RUMINANT An animal that regurgitates its food and chews it again (known as "chewing the cud").

SALIVA A thin, watery liquid secreted by salivary glands in the mouth to soften food and prepare it for digestion.

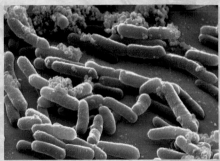
Micrograph of salmonella

SALMONELLA A large group of rod-shaped bacteria, many of which are associated with food poisoning.

SALTING A method of food preservation using large amounts of salt.

SATURATED FAT A fat that is usually solid at room temperature. For example, butter, lard, and palm and coconut oil.

SIMPLE CARBOHYDRATE Sugars, such as naturally-occurring lactose (milk sugar) and fructose (in fruit and honey), as well as processed sugars such as sucrose (table sugar). They are easily converted to glucose.

SMALL INTESTINE A long tube beneath the stomach in which food is broken down and absorbed during digestion.

SOLUBLE Capable of being dissolved.

STOMACH The strong, muscular bag into which food flows from the oesophagus. The stomach churns food and mixes it with enzymes.

TOXIC Containing a poisonous substance.

UNSATURATED FAT A fat which is usually liquid at room temperature.

VEGAN DIET A diet that consists only of plant foods.

VEGETARIANISM A diet that is based on plant foods, with or without animal-based foods, such as dairy products, eggs, and honey.

VILLI A fingerlike projection in the small intestine through which food is absorbed.

VITAMIN Any of the organic substances that are essential in small quantities to the nutrition of most animals and some plants.

Index

Acknowledgements

Indexer: Hilary Bird

Picture credits:
The publisher would like to thank the following for their kind permission to reproduce their photographs.
a=above, b=bottom/below, c=centre, l=left, r=right, t=top

3 Getty Images: AFP. 4 DK Images: Clive Streeter © DK Courtesy of the Science Museum, London (cr). 6 Corbis: H. David Seawell (tl). 7 Photolibrary.com: OSF (bl); Science Photo Library: Susumu Nishinaga (bc). 8 Science Photo Library: Dr. Arthur Tucker (tl); Zefa Visual Media: Michael W. Davidson (crb); Still Pictures: I. Uwanaka/UNEP (tr); Topfoto.co.uk: (br). 10 Corbis: William Sallaz (b); DK Images: Clive Streeter © DK Courtesy of the Science Museum, London (cr); Mary Evans Picture Library: (tl). 11 Science Photo Library: Dr. Tim Evans (tr), Mehau Kulyk (bl). 12 Mary Evans Picture Library: (cl). 14 ImageState/Pictor: (bc). 15 Alamy Images: (tr); ImageState/Pictor: Paddy Eckersley (b). 16 Corbis: Charles & Josette Lenras (cr). 17 Empics Ltd: (b); Hulton Archive/ Getty Images: (cl). Science Photo Library: CNRI (tl), David Scharf (cla). 18 Mary Evans Picture Library: (tl). 19 DK Images: David Jordan © The Ivy Press Limited (b); Science Photo Library: Dr. Jeremy Burgess (tl). 20 Mary Evans Picture Library: (tl); Science Photo Library: Charles D. Winters (tr). 21 Corbis: Galen Rowell (tr), Patrik Giardino (b); Science Photo Library: Biophoto Associates (ca), Michael W. Davidson (tl). 22 www.bridgeman.co.uk: (tl); Corbis: Bettmann (tr); Science Photo Library: Cristina Pedrazzini (bl), D. Phillips (cr hair), Ken Eward/Biografx (cl), VVG (cr skin). 24 Mary

Evans Picture Library: (tl); Science Photo Library: David Parker (bl), prof. P. Motta/Dept of Anatomy/University "La Sapienza", Rome (bc), Thomas Hollyman (br). 25 Corbis: Ed bock (tl); DK Images: Guy Ryecart & David Jordan © The Ivy Press Limited (c); Science Photo Library: Mark Clarke (br), Michael W. Davidson (tr.); ImageState/Pictor: (crb). 26 Mary Evans Picture Library: (tr.); Science Photo Library: Andrew Syred (tr), (cl); Still Pictures: SOMBOON-UNEP (br). 28 Science Photo Library: Dr. Tony Brain (tr). 29 Pictures Colour Library: (cr); Topfoto.co.uk: (tr); Zefa Visual Media: Sucré Salé/J.Riou (l). 30 Corbis: James Marshall (bl). 31 Corbis: Philip Gould (br); Science Photo Library: (cla), Astrid & Hanns-Frieder Michler (ca), Claude Nuridsany & Marie Perennou (tl), Profs P.M. Motta & F.M. Magliocca (cb); Still Pictures: Markus Dlouhy (cr). 32 Corbis: Bettmann (bl), (br); Getty Images: Christoph Wilhelm (tl); Science Photo Library: CNRI (tc), (ca). 33 Science Photo Library: Eye of Science (bc), Prof Cinti & V. Gremet (tl), Scott Camazine (tc). 34 Alamy Images: Julia Martin (tr). 35 ImageState/Pictor: Adrian Peacock (cr); Science Photo Library: Dr. P. Marazzi (bc). 36 Alamy Images: B & Y Photography (tr); Corbis: Bettmann (br), Chris Hellier (cr). 37 Getty Images: Hulton Archive/Getty Images (tr); Powerstock: Superstock (l); Science Photo Library: NASA (cr), Sidney Moulds (br). 38 DK Images: Peter Anderson © Danish National Museum (tr); The Natural History Museum, London: (tl). 39 Alamy Images: Popperfoto (cl); Corbis: David Papazian (br), Stapleton Collection (clb). 40 The Art Archive: Biblioteca Nazionale Marciana Venice/Dagli Orti (br); Photolibrary.com: Zhanquan Sun (b); Topfoto.co.uk: (tr). 41 Alamy Images: Photo Japan (tl); Still Pictures: Jochen Tack (br); Topfoto.co.uk: (cl). 42 Alamy Images:

(bc); Corbis: Caroline Penn (br), Reuters (cr); DK Images: The British Library (tr); Lonely Planet Images: Alan Benson (cl). 43 www.bridgeman. co.uk: Begg, Samuel (fl. 1886-1916)/The Illustrated London News Picture Library, London, UK (tr); Corbis: Frank Leather/Eye Ubiquitous (b); Photolibrary.com: Steven Mark Needham (cl). 44 DK Images: National Museums of Scotland (bl); Eye Ubiquitous: Chris Fairclough (clb). 44 Impact Photos: (crb); Lonely Planet Images: Sara-Jane Cleland (tl). 45 Corbis: Archivo Iconografico, S.A. (cla); Getty Images: AFP (b). 46 Alamy Images: Justine Kase (cl); Topfoto.co.uk: The Image Works (r). 47 Corbis: Bettmann (cl), Joseph Sohm; Chromosohm Inc. (tl); The Art Archive: São Paulo Art Museum Brazil/Dagli Orti (c); Getty Images: Donna Day (tr); Time Life Pictures (bl); Rex Features: Chat (cr), Ross Hodgson (br). 48 Corbis: Bettmann (cl), Joseph Sohm; DK Images: Geoff Brightling, Courtesy of the Museum of English Rural Life, The University of Reading (tl). 49 Corbis: Paul Almasy (tl), Peter Beck (b), Richard A. Cooke (tr). 50 DK Images: Geoff Brightling, Courtesy of the Museum of English Rural Life, University of Reading (l). 50-51 Corbis: Farrell Grehan (t). 51 Alamy Images: Hal Brindley/ VWPICS (br); Eye Ubiquitous: Sue Passmore (tr); Getty Images: John & Eliza Forder (cr); Rex Features: Times Newspapers (tl). 52 Mary Evans Picture Library: (tl), (tr); Science Photo Library: Mauro Fermariello (cl). 52-53 Alamy Images: Joseph Sohm (b). 53 Alamy Images: (cr), Nick Simon (t); DK Images: Geoff Brightling, Courtesy of the Museum of English Rural Life, The University of Reading (l); Lonely Planet Images: Alan Benson (b). 54 Corbis: Lindsay Hebberd (cla); DK Images: British Museum (tl). 55 Corbis: Michael S. Yamashita (b); Science Photo Library: Simon Fraser (cra). 56 Corbis:

Michael S. Yamashita (c), Tom Nebbia (bl); Science Photo Library: Simon Fraser/Royal Victoria Infirmary, Newcastle Upon Tyne (tl); Still Pictures: Harmut Scwarzbach (crb); Sebastian Bolesch (tr). 57 Alamy Images: Bill Barksdale (cr) Shout (tr); Corbis: Don Mason (b); Science Photo Library: Barry Dowsett (tl). 58 Corbis: Bettmann (tl); Science Photo Library: Martyn F. Chillmaid (cra), Peter Menzel (c). 58-59 Alamy Images: Chris Knapton. 59 Science Photo Library: Biology Media (tc), Dr. Tim Evans (b); Still Pictures: Nick Cobbing (tr). 60 Getty Images: Time Life Pictures (tl). 60-61 Alamy Images: (b). 61 DK Images: Guy Ryecart, The Ivy Press (br). Still Pictures: Martin Bond (b), Paul Glendell (tl), Pierre Gleizes (tr). 62 The Art Archive: Museo Correr Venice/Dagli Orti (tl); Still Pictures: Hartmut Schwarzbach (cra); Topfoto.co.uk: (clb). 62-63 Pa Photos: EPA. 63 Eye Ubiquitous: Hutchison Library: Crispin Hughes (br), Trevor Page (tr); Still Pictures: Klein/Hubert (b). 64 DK Images: Steve Gorton, courtesy of Booth Museum of Natural History, Brighton (bl). Robert Harding Picture Library: Advertasia (bc); Still Pictures: Harmut Schwarzbach (tl). 65 Corbis: Bettmann (tr), Reuters (br). 66 akg-images: (tl); DK Images: Philip Dowell (b). 67 The Advertising Archive: (br); Corbis: Lake County Museum (tr). 68 Corbis: Ariel Skelley (b), Vittoriano Rastelli (r). 69 Alamy Images: Andre Jenny (tr); DK Images: Peter Hayman © The British Museum (bc); Science Photo Library: Cordelia Molloy (br). 70 Science Photo Library: (t). 70-71 Science Photo Library: Prof. K. Seddon & Dr. T. Evans, Queen's University Belfast (c). 71 Science Photo Library: Eye of Science (tr).

All other images © DK Images.com